PHalarope Books

PHalarope Books are designed specifically for the amateur naturalist.
These volumes represent excellence in natural history publishing. Most books in the
PHalarope series are based on a nature course or program at the college or adult
education level or are sponsored by a museum or nature center. Each PHalarope
book reflects the author's teaching ability as well as writing ability.
Among the books:

THE AMATEUR NATURALIST'S HANDBOOK
Vinson Brown

BOTANY IN THE FIELD:
An Introduction to Plant Communities for the Amateur Naturalist
Jane Scott

THE CURIOUS NATURALIST
John Mitchell and the Massachusetts Audubon Society

A FIELD GUIDE TO THE FAMILIAR:
Learning to Observe the Natural World
Gale Lawrence

INSECT LIFE:
A Field Entomology Manual for the Amateur Naturalist
Ross H. Arnett, Jr., and Richard L. Jacques, Jr.

A NATURAL HISTORY OF PLANTS:
An Illustrated Botanical Primer for Naturalists, Gardeners, and Artists
Jorie Hunken

NATURE DRAWING:
A Tool for Learning
Clare Walker Leslie

THE PLANT OBSERVER'S GUIDEBOOK:
A Field Botany Manual for the Amateur Naturalist
Charles E. Roth

POND AND BROOK:
A Guide to Nature Study in Freshwater Environments
Michael J. Caduto

SUBURBAN WILDFLOWERS:
An Introduction to the Common Wildflowers of Your
Back Yard and Local Park
Richard Headstrom

THOREAU'S METHOD:
A Handbook for Nature Study
David Pepi

TREES:
An Introduction to Trees and Forest Ecology for the Amateur Naturalist
Laurence C. Walker

❧ THE JOY OF WILDFLOWERS

THE JOY OF WILDFLOWERS

A Fieldbook of Familiar Flowers of Rural and Urban Habitats in the Eastern United States

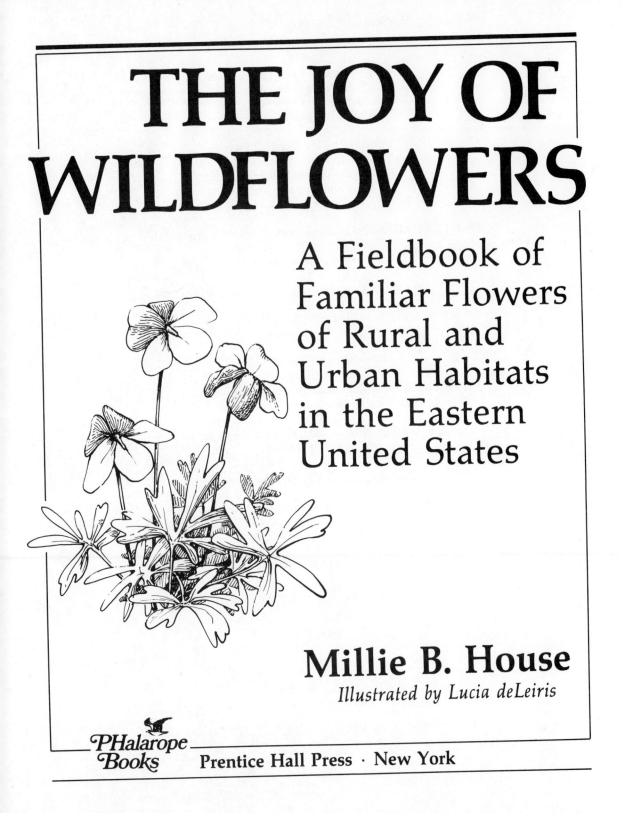

Millie B. House

Illustrated by Lucia deLeiris

PHalarope Books

Prentice Hall Press · New York

Published by Prentice Hall Press
A Division of Simon & Schuster, Inc.
Gulf+Western Building
One Gulf+Western Plaza
New York, NY 10023

PRENTICE HALL PRESS is a trademark of Simon & Schuster, Inc.

PHalarope Books

Library of Congress Cataloging in Publication Data

House, Millie B.
The joy of wildflowers.

Bibliography: p.
Includes index.
1. Wild flowers—Northeastern States—Identification.
2. Wild flowers—Northeastern States—Habitat.
I. Title.
QK118.H64 1986   582.13'0974   86-5081
ISBN 0-13-511635-X

Designed by Irving Perkins Associates

Manufactured in the United States of America

10 9 8 7 6 5 4 3 2 1

First Edition

For my grandchildren
Jamie, Kriss, and Jed

ACKNOWLEDGMENTS

I AM DEEPLY INDEBTED to the following:

Harriet Jackson Phelps of Newport, Rhode Island, and Camden, South Carolina, introduced me many years ago to the fun of botanizing. We have spent many hours in the field, forest, and wetlands looking for both the common and the rare.

Martha Marshall has spent many a Saturday riding the back roads to find roadside as well as field and forest plants. June Buyea of Tiverton, Rhode Island, and formerly of Bradford, Vermont, introduced me to the beauties of the North Country.

Richard Champlin of the Redwood Library, Newport, Rhode Island, and Rick Ensor and Chris Raithel of the Department of Environmental Management of the State of Rhode Island gave me their advice.

Mr. and Mrs. R. F. Haffenraffer III, allowed me to use their beautiful acres of woods, fields, wetlands, and shores for study. The Haffenraffer Museum of Brown University also allowed me the use of their acreage.

Without Ellen Wilson's moral support, I would never have finished. Valorie Catalano generously gave of her time to retype the manuscript.

Mary Kennan, editor, had faith in me.

My daughter and a talented artist, Cindy House, introduced me to the bogs and rock shores of Maine.

CONTENTS

FOREWORD   xiii

PREFACE   xv

1 · STARTING OUT   1

2 · URBAN WILDFLOWERS: *A City Stroll*   5

3 · SEA BEACHES   15

4 · BOGS   23

5 · SALT MARSHES   33

6 · WOODLANDS: *Early Spring*   41

7 · WOODLANDS: *Midsummer*   55

8 · WOODLANDS: *Late Summer*   63

9 · WETLANDS: *Spring*   71

10 · WETLANDS: *Midsummer*   77

11 · WETLANDS: *Late Summer*   87

12 · **PONDS AND BROOKS:** *Aquatic Plants*   95

13 · **OPEN FIELDS**   103

14 · **FIELD FLOWERS:** *Early Summer*   107

15 · **FIELD FLOWERS:** *Midsummer—June*   113

16 · **FIELD FLOWERS:** *Midsummer—July*   121

17 · **FIELD FLOWERS:** *Late Summer*   131

18 · **FIELD FLOWERS:** *Autumn*   137

19 · **ROADSIDES**   141

BIBLIOGRAPHY   153

INDEX   155

FOREWORD

FROM SIDEWALK CRACKS AND abandoned city lots to luxuriant climatic forests, wildflowers are readily available from six to eight months of the year in the New England area, and almost throughout the year further south. They are an ever-present reminder of nature's awe-inspiring creativity. The identification of the numerous species is not only one of the most exciting pastimes, but is also a necessary exercise if we are going to preserve our native flora. Awareness of the beauty of wildflowers, the fragility of their environments, and their role in food chains will contribute to the healthy maintenance of this precious legacy to future generations. Thus, any book which attempts to simplify plant identification as well as enhance the reader's appreciation for wildflowers is indeed welcome.

The novice wildflower enthusiast has many books from which to choose. Some of these utilize traditional scientific classification, while others group flowers according to color, time of bloom, or even economic and medicinal uses. These approaches, however, are often confusing for the beginning student.

After many years of teaching high-school and college-level courses in natural history and trying to simplify plant identification for her students, Millie House has devised a guide to the wildflowers of the Northeast in which the plants are grouped according to habitats. These include beaches, dunes, bogs, salt marshes, wetlands, roadsides, vacant lots, open fields, woodlands, and mountains. When appropriate, the plants within each habitat are divided into blooming periods: April–May, June–July, and August–September. Grouping the plants according to *where* they are likely to be found and *when* they will bloom will greatly facilitate exploration and eliminate errors at the start. The initial choices involved in the identification process, thus simplified, should therefore encourage the beginner for whom this book is designed.

The Joy of Wildflowers is a pleasure to read. The descriptions of the plants include information on habitat, range, use, and other pertinent botanical facts and comments. The text contains a minimum of technical terms and the vocabulary is easy to understand. Scientific names are used as well as common ones and are based on the eighth edition (1950) of *Gray's Manual of Botany*.

The countless hours Millie has spent on field trips, either driving along roadsides, or walking over precarious trails looking for rare species, have given her a truly encyclopedic knowledge of our native flora. She knows exactly where to find Whorled Pogonias or any species of fringed orchid, but will only divulge their locations if she is assured that the plants will not be disturbed. In this book, her love of nature, her incessant curiosity, and her concern for native plant protection are self-evident. This guide will prove helpful to many and should become an indispensable field tool for the wildflower explorer.

Martine Villalard-Bohnsack
Professor of Biology
Roger Williams College,
Bristol, Rhode Island

PREFACE

I CAN THINK OF NO better hobby than wildflower identification. No matter where in the world you are apt to go, you will find a flower with enough determination to grow even in the cracks of a sidewalk. I have always said that wildflowers, growing in incredible sizes, shapes, and colors, are the frosting on nature's landscape. You need no fancy equipment other than a hand lens, because sometimes flowers are very small and can best be seen under magnification. A field guide—today there are many written for the individual states or for large areas—and a good pair of walking shoes or even boots for sloshing around in wet places are indispensable. Of course, a sunny day would be nice, but you can see almost as much on a cloudy day. However, there are a few flowers that close up on a sunless day.

When it comes to wildflowers, most people know a dandelion from a daisy and a buttercup from a violet. These are interesting common flowers. The dandelion is made up of hundreds of threadlike disk flowers, and the daisy is made up of a tight center of yellow disk flowers and a rim of white ray flowers surrounding the center. These characteristics are very useful in helping to identify other flowers.

Our American landscape is carpeted with wildflowers at varying times of the year, depending upon both the season and the location—whether it is north, south, east, or west, mountains or desert, wetlands or seashore, woodlands or fields. We will explore the common wildflowers of the northeast quadrant of the United States. From the earliest spring days, when the skunk cabbage comes in bloom, to the last dull day of fall, the search for wildflowers is a rewarding experience that often leads to in-depth study, as it did in my case.

The object of this book is to introduce the novice to the common wildflowers, their habitats, and times of bloom. The general consensus is that there are about 10,000 species of wildflowers in the United States alone, so be assured you will never run out of new worlds to conquer.

In times past wildflowers were an essential part of life. Food, medicines, dyes, symbols, perfumes, cording or rope, and thatching for roofs were but a few of their uses. Today, many of these uses are still valid. And wild animals depend on seeds, roots, nectar, and leaves for food. Alas, for so many people, wildflowers are just a spot of color on the landscape. *Stop* and *investigate.* If my book does not have the answer, try others. There is a list at the end of the book that I have used and recommend.

Happy botanizing.

STARTING OUT

MY APPROACH TO THIS BOOK is a little different. The emphasis will be on ecological areas or habitats. If you do not know what a habitat is, a good definition is "the place where you live."

Since there are so many factors that control flowering, there is continuous blooming from March to November in the northeast quadrant of the United States. That quadrant is the focus of this book, although many of the flowers you will meet can be found in other regions of North America as well. Some of the flowers are discussed more than once because they may be found in more than one area.

We will start with the earliest spring flowers in a habitat and work through fall to the frost. Some areas, such as the sea beach, do not have any spring flowers. And there are a few shrubs that cannot be left out by virtue of the fact that they are associated with certain wild flowers or habitats.

Many of the woodland plants must bloom before the canopy of the forest has leafed out, while the sun can reach the forest floor.

Field flowers take advantage of the long, sunny days of summer, while the fall flowers are favored with an extra-long growing season. If a spring has been unduly dark and cool, there are some plants that will skip blooming altogether, since they have not been able to store enough food in their roots to produce blooms.

By and large, most plants respond to their particular needs and bloom on time, depending upon latitude, altitude, soil, rainfall or dryness, heat, and cold. The farther north you go, the later the leafing and blooming. A friend here in southern New England, who used to summer in Vermont, always said she had the advantage of two springs.

Obviously spring does not occur at the same time across the country. Basically it marches northward at the rate of 15 miles per day. On mountainsides it rises at the rate of 100 feet per day.

The enchantment of spring has been the subject of song and story, and to watch its magic can be one of life's most rewarding experiences. If you are a beginning flower sleuth, do not be discouraged if you cannot identify all the plants, because with patience it will all crystallize.

You might want to keep a record of what you see, and in that case, a small plant press will be very handy. Lacking that, an old telephone book is an excellent press. When you press flowers, place them carefully so that they look at you. Spread the leaves so that they are readily identifiable. Put some kind of a weight on the closed book and keep it in a warm place for about a week. Your neatly pressed flowers can then easily be mounted on paper by using a thin paste. You can also cover them with clear contact paper. Be sure to identify your plant and where you found it, as well as the date.

Where the flowers are plentiful, it will do no harm to pick one. However, where the plant is listed as rare or endangered, it should never be picked, and I repeat: *never be picked.* Most states issue lists of the rare flowers in their area and the laws governing them.

Most flowers are made up of four parts. Petals are the colorful and eye-catching part of the flower and are arranged around the main stem either regularly or irregularly. Sepals, found under the petals, actually cap the petals before they bloom and are usually green, but in some cases the sepals act as petals and are colorful. Above the petals, and arranged around the stem, are threadlike stamens with pollen anthers at the ends. These may be numerous or few. The stamen is the male organ of the flower. Rising out of the center is the pistil, a stalk with a knob on the end, sometimes divided. This is the female organ. At the base of the pistil is the swollen ovary that will contain the seeds if the flower is pollinated.

Some flowers do not contain all four parts. Some may have no pistils or may contain only stamens; some may have no petals. These are called imperfect flowers. The flowers that contain only stamens are called staminate, and those that contain only pistils are called pistillate. However, both may be found on the same plant or on separate plants.

Some plants are perennial, coming up from the same root year after year. Some are annual and must depend on the last year's harvest of seeds for growing and blooming.

Plants, like all living organisms, fall into families; there are 303 identified plant families. A family is the large, overall related group that is further broken down into genus (plural, genera) and species, both of which are given Latin names. Genus is a more closely related group, and species is a particular kind of plant with no other like it. Plants, like all other organisms, are given two Latin names, the genus and the species. A plant will have only one Latin name, but it may have many common names.

Leaves also come in many shapes and sizes as well as designs. Some leaves are sessile, which means that they are joined directly to the stem. Some are compound, which means that the leaf is made up of smaller leaflets. Some are palmate, and look like your hand with your fingers spread apart. Leaves may be placed alternately on the stem or they may be opposite. They may be whorled around the stem. They may be long and narrow, lanceolate or broad, or egg-shaped. They may be in the shape of an arrowhead or heart-shaped. The surface may be smooth or rough as sandpaper. The color of leaves can range from dusty white to deep green.

So, to begin wildflower watching, that's enough to know. Bring a small notebook, a pencil, perhaps a hand lens or magnifying glass—and your favorite field guide—and come wildflower walking with me.

2

URBAN WILDFLOWERS

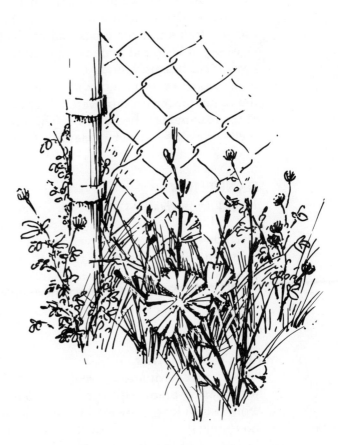

A City Stroll

I N MOST OF OUR CITIES there are vacant lots that at one time were the sites of houses, stores, or other buildings that were destroyed by fire or vandals, or torn down. These areas have been left to their own devices. Generally, the soil is poor, but nature sets to work to cover the scars. There are plants that have an affinity for places like this. Their seeds are often borne on the wind or dropped by birds. When they settle down with the help of rain, they start to sprout. Gradually the vacant lot takes on a covering of green.

Coarse grasses and sedges as well as wildflowers will spring up here. Most of the wildflowers are native to Europe or Asia but have become established in this country. Of course the flowers are also found in open fields and roadsides. Not all urban wildflowers can be found in one lot nor at the same time, but once in a while rarities are found.

A number of years ago, while driving along a railroad track in the center of a city, I discovered Tarweed growing along the side of the road next to the sidewalk. This plant is from the West. The seeds probably hitched a ride on a train.

DANDELION

Taraxacum officinale—COMPOSITE FAMILY. Probably one of the first to bloom is the ubiquitous dandelion. Most of us know it. The flower is a compact, yellow disk flower 1½ inches wide, found on a single bare stem rising from a basal rosette of deeply lobed leaves. It can grow up to 18 inches in height. It ranges over much of the country except in the Southeast. Before it flowers, the green leaves can be gathered as a pot herb and used in salad.

BLACK MUSTARD

Brassica nigra—MUSTARD FAMILY. A tall spike about 2 feet in height, many branched, with small, four-petaled yellow flowers, about ½ inch long, growing in masses at the end of the stem. The interesting thing about these flowers is that they start to bloom at the bottom of the stem, the main stem rising out of the basal rosette of shiny, lobed leaves. It is found over most of America except in the Southwest. The leaves and flowers can be cooked and eaten as greens. For many years immigrants to our country combed the fields and vacant lots, gathering these plants for food.

COMMON MULLEIN

Verbascum thapsus—SNAPDRAGON FAMILY. One of the tallest plants found in waste places, this plant is a biennial, which means it takes two years to flower. The individual flowers are found running up a coarse stem that reaches a height of 6 feet. The flowers have five petals and are bright yellow, 1 inch wide, and rather flat. The leaves are the interesting thing about this plant: they are large—up to 12 inches long—oblong, and velvety in texture. The gray-green leaves are in a basal rosette which comes up in the spring, and winters until the following spring when the plant sends up a main stem on which flowers are borne. They bloom all summer and are found over most of the United States. The leaves have had many uses in the past; they were used medicinally for colds, various respiratory problems, and other ailments. The leaves dry beautifully and can be used in dried arrangements.

YARROW

Achillea millefolium—COMPOSITE FAMILY. This flower grows from 1 to 3 feet tall with a single, flat cluster of tiny gray-white flowers, ¼ inch wide, found at the end of the stem. The gray-green, aromatic leaves are finely divided, almost fernlike, and grow to 6 inches in length. The plant blooms from July to September, and was once thought to have medicinal properties. It is still used by people who practice herbal medicine.

COMMON TANSY

Tanacetum vulgare—COMPOSITE FAMILY. Another tall plant of waste places, which grows up to 4 feet or more in height. At the top of the straight stem is a flat cluster of buttonlike, bright-yellow flowers. Tansy also has aromatic leaves that are about 8

COMMON TANSY
Its bitter leaves once typified the bitter herbs eaten in Lent. Often the leaves were used in confections.

inches long and deeply serrated; the individual leaflets are also serrated. It blooms all summer, into fall, and is well established all over the United States and Canada. For a long time this plant was used medicinally; however, it is toxic and may have killed more than it cured.

CHICKORY

Cichorium intybus—COMPOSITE FAMILY.   Again, a tall plant with a stiff stem up to 4 feet in height. Its blue flowers grow up the stem singularly and adhere directly to it. Each flower is 1 to 1½ inches across and is composed of numerous ray flowers. The petals are square and serrated. Chickory blooms early in the morning and fades with the heat of the noonday sun. The stem rises out of a basal rosette of leaves, not unlike dandelion, up to 6 inches in length. The leaves can be cooked and eaten early in the spring. The root, when dried, ground up, and roasted, can be used as a coffee substitute. Chickory is found throughout the whole area and blooms all summer into the fall.

COMMON BURDOCK

Arctium minus—COMPOSITE FAMILY.   Probably the coarsest plant you will find in an abandoned area. A tall plant, 4 feet or more, its flowers adhere directly to the stem and are pinkish-lavender with threadlike petals. They are enclosed in a prickly outer covering, which, when dry, is a nuisance because it sticks to anything that touches it, whether the fur of an animal or clothing. Its leaves are huge—up to 18 inches long around the base of the stem and becoming smaller toward the top of the stem. Burdock is found across Canada, south through New England to Georgia, west to Mississippi, and north to Kansas. The root and early leaves are considered good eating.

WHITE CAMPION or EVENING LYCHNIS

Lychnis alba—PINK FAMILY.   Often seen in vacant lots, it blooms in the early evening, but may also be found in the daytime. The plant is from 1 to 3 feet tall with white flowers, although they are sometimes pink. The five petals are deeply notched. The plant has both male and female flowers: males have ten stamens and the females have five styles. The base of the flower is inflated. The leaves are velvety, lanceolate, and 1 to 4 inches long. It is found from Quebec through New England to South Carolina, west to Alabama, and north to Missouri. Campion blooms from July into October.

COMMON MILKWEED

Asclepias syriaca—MILKWEED FAMILY.   A tall, rather coarse plant with clusters of five small downward-pointing petals, pink, brown, or purple, growing at the end of a 1-inch-long stem. Its leaves are large, from 4 to 10 inches in length, broadly oval, light green, and velvety underneath. It blooms from June to August. The very early shoots in the spring can be eaten as a vegetable, but caution should be taken as the plant is toxic. It grows from southern Canada through New England to Georgia, and west to Kansas. Its seeds are rather spectacular in the fall, since they attach to bits of fluff called parachutes, which help the wind to carry them away.

RAGWEED

Ambrosia artemisiifolia—COMPOSITE FAMILY.   This is one of the most obnoxious weeds in vacant lots because its pollen causes severe allergic reactions in some people. You would *not* want to pick a ragweed bouquet. The plant contains both male and female flowers; the male flower is the more conspicuous with its copious pollen. It ranges in height up to 5 feet, with a coarse stem that is branched near the top. The male flowers are found on the small stems and are like tiny buttons of yellow pollen with no petals; this pollen is windblown. The female flowers are tiny, green, and found in clusters at the junction of the leaf and stem. The leaves are up to 4 inches long, fernlike and deeply serrated. Ragweed is found throughout the area and blooms from July to September.

BULL THISTLE

Cirsium vulgare—COMPOSITE FAMILY.   This is a tall plant, growing up to 6 feet. Its flowers are rather showy: purple-rose in color and composed of disk flowers only, in a compact head about 2 inches in diameter encircled by thorny bracts. The leaves are up to 6 inches in length, coarsely serrated and thorny. It is a biennal, producing a basal rosette of thorny leaves the first year and a tall flowering stem the next year. Attached to its seeds are fluffy parachutes called thistledown, used by birds to line their nests. It blooms from July to September and is found throughout the area.

PEPPER GRASS

Lepidium virginicum—MUSTARD FAMILY.   It is a weedy plant found in most vacant lots. The white flowers are hardly visible, only $\frac{1}{12}$ inch across, with four petals terminating the stem in a cluster. The leaves are basals up to 2 inches long, and serrated with a large lobe at the end. Pepper Grass is found throughout the area and blooms from June to November. The seeds have a peppery taste and can be used for seasoning.

WHITE SWEET CLOVER

Melilotus alba—PEA FAMILY.   A tall member of the pea family, it can reach a height of 8 feet. The flowers are small, white, and pealike, arranged closely up the stem in a spike. The flowers are ¼ inch long. The leaves are in threes, lanceolate and serrated. Sweet clover blooms all summer and generally grows in waste places. It is highly valued as a honey-producing plant.

YELLOW SWEET CLOVER

Melilotus officinalis—PEA FAMILY.   Very similar to the previous except that it is not as tall, only reaching 5 feet, and the flowers are yellow. These two plants are often found growing together.

YELLOW HAWKWEED

Hieracium pratense—COMPOSITE FAMILY.   The flowers, yellow and dandelionlike, cluster at the end of a hairy stem rising out of a rosette of leaves 2 to 10 inches long. The leaves are oblong and covered with bristly hairs. The plant is 1 to 3 feet in height and blooms from May to September. It is found from southern Canada through Nova Scotia to New England and south to the higher elevations in Georgia.

There is a bright red-orange species, *Hieracium aurantiacum*, very much like the yellow species except for its color; it grows in similar places. It blooms from June to September and is found from Newfoundland to West Virginia, and north to Minnesota. Both of these flowers are considered weeds, but they are colorful.

PRICKLY LETTUCE

Lactuca scariola—COMPOSITE FAMILY.   Found in waste places, it is a tall plant, up to 5 feet, and widely branched at the end of the main stem. Terminating the branches are small, yellow dandelionlike flowers, ¼ inch wide. The leaves are oblong, lobed or unlobed, with bristly ribs and edges. A milky fluid seeps from a break in any part of the plant. It is found throughout most of the United States and blooms from June to October.

SMOOTH SUMAC

Rhus glabra—CASHEW FAMILY. This is not really considered a wildflower, but is often found growing in corners of vacant lots. It is a shrub, growing up to 10 feet or more, with tiny, greenish-yellow flowers found terminally in pyramid-shaped clusters. Its leaves are compound, with serrated leaflets up to 4 inches long. Its velvety, red fruit and its brilliant fall foliage are its hallmarks. Smooth sumac is not poisonous and is found throughout the area.

QUEEN ANNE'S LACE

Daucus carota—PARSLEY FAMILY. The flowers are found at the stem of this plant, which can grow up to 4 feet in height. They are made up of dull-white, flat-topped clusters, about 3 to 4 inches in diameter, in a lacy radial pattern. Its leaves are finely divided and fernlike, up to 8 inches long. Queen Anne's lace is found throughout the area. They are sometimes called "bird's nests," because when the flowers have gone to seed, the dried flowers curl up to the center and resemble a bird's nest.

CURLY DOCK

Rumex crispus—BUCKWHEAT FAMILY. This is also a tall, coarse plant, branched near the top of the main stem. The individual flowers are very tiny, ⅙ inch long, greenish-pink, and growing in whorls around and up the stem. The leaves are large, up to 10 inches long, lanceolate, and wavy along the edges. The flowers produce brown seeds which are often used in flower arrangements. It is said that the early spring leaves can be used as a salad green; however, dock is bitter.

BUTTER-AND-EGGS

Linaria vulgaris—SNAPDRAGON FAMILY. Butter-and-eggs is an irregular, snapdragonlike flower in two shades of yellow, about 1 inch long including a long spur. It grows on a single slender stem which can reach up to 3 feet in height. The leaves are gray-green and threadlike, growing closely to the stem. It is found throughout the whole area and blooms from May to October.

CELANDINE
Chelidonium majus—POPPY FAMILY. The flower is a cluster of four bright-yellow petals about 1 inch wide. Celandine is found from New England, south to Georgia, and west to Missouri; they bloom from April to August. Like most members of the poppy family, a broken branch will ooze a fluid, in this case yellow.

SMARTWEED or PINK KNOTWEED
Polygonum pensylvanicum—BUCKWHEAT FAMILY. The flowers of this plant are very tiny, ⅛ inch long, and grow terminally on the upper branching stems in tight masses. The flowers do not have any petals, only colored sepals. The stems are joined, and the leaves are lanceolate. Smartweed blooms all summer and is found throughout the area.

EVENING PRIMROSE
Oenothera biennis—EVENING PRIMROSE FAMILY. As the name suggests, it is a biennial flower, blooming the second year of its life. Its flowers are 1 to 1½ inches across, with four yellow petals growing in a group toward the end of a sturdy stem. The leaves are lanceolate, up to 8 inches long. These plants bloom all summer and are found throughout the area.

HORSEWEED
Erigeron canadensis—COMPOSITE FAMILY. This is a rough-stemmed plant, branching toward the top of the main stem with clusters of tiny, greenish-white flowers, ½ inch long. The flowers do not spread out, but form small tubes. The leaves are dark green and linear, 4 inches long. This plant blooms from July to November and is found everywhere.

BUSHY ASTER
Aster dumosus—COMPOSITE FAMILY. There are many species of asters. The white bushy aster seems to like to grow in abandoned

places. It is, as its name suggests, a stiff, bushy plant with numerous branching stems. Its tiny, white, daisylike flowers, ½ to ⅔ inch wide, grow terminally on the stem. Sometimes the flower is lavender or pale blue. Its leaves are lanceolate, 3 inches in length. It can grow up to 3 feet tall and blooms from August to October. It is found from southeast Ontario through New England to Florida, west to Texas, and north to Michigan. Often it will hybridize with other asters and become hard to identify.

SEA BEACHES

WE WILL CONTINUE OUR WILDFLOWER-WATCHING adventure by walking along a sea beach. From Cape Cod across southern New England, and south, there is almost a continous line of beaches of fine sand made up of hard minerals such as quartz, feldspar, magnetite, and garnet, and also bits of shells of invertebrates that inhabit the sea below the high-tide line.

Most plants cannot grow in salt water because they have no ability to absorb salt; therefore, they have to be out of the reach of the fingers of the sea. However, there are a number of factors which control the growth on the sea beach just above the high-tide line, allowing plants to make use of whatever fresh water is available. The controlling factors are wind, salt air, temperature, and salt spray. The winds blow almost constantly along the beach, shifting the sand and in some places creating dunes.

Nature has designed a group of plants that can make use of whatever water is available. Some plants have fleshy leaves where fresh water can be stored. Some plants are covered with a dusty coating which inhibits desiccation. Some have long, tenacious roots reaching down through the damp sand to the water table. It may surprise you to know that there are a number of species that can grow and bloom just above the wrack line. None of these have large bright flowers, and many are so small that it is hard to see them. There seem to be no early spring flowers; most bloom in midsummer.

SEA ROCKET

Cakile edentula—MUSTARD FAMILY.   Probably the most common is this fleshy plant, 6 to 12 inches in height. The leaves are thick, fleshy, 1 inch long, serrated, and narrowing where the leaf joins the main stem. The flowers have four petals that grow out of the main stem. They are lavender and about ¼ inch across. When the flowers go to seed, they form an interesting capsule which, when ripe, will drop on the shore and be moved around by the sea. They are found all along the Atlantic seacoast and along the shores of the Great Lakes.

ORACH or SPEARSCALE

Atriplex patula—GOOSEFOOT FAMILY. Often among the Sea Rocket we will see this plant, which can grow up to 3 feet tall. Its leaves are often triangular or arrow-shaped. Some leaves are smooth along the edges, while others are slightly serrated and covered with a mealy bloom. The tiny green flowers grow on spikes from the junction of the leaf and the stem. Like all sea-beach flowers, they bloom in the summer and the early fall. As well as along the beach, Orach can be found in saline or alkaline soil elsewhere. It can be cooked as a pot herb, but do not salt it as it has a built-in salt shaker.

SEABEACH ORACH

Atriplex arenaria—GOOSEFOOT FAMILY. This species is very much like the *Atriplex patula*, but it is only found growing on the beach from New Hampshire south. Instead of arrow-shaped leaves, it has oblong leaves, also covered with whitish bloom. The flowers are found above leaves which are often red in color, at the leaf junctions toward the top of the stem.

SEASIDE SPURGE

Euphorbia polygonifolia—EUPHORBIA FAMILY. Walking along the sand, you may come to this small, sprawling plant whose branches grow in all directions. Its tiny leaves are leathery, about ¼ inch long, and grow on red stems. The flowers are very small, but believe it or not, its seeds are larger than its leaves. It is related to the Christmas Poinsettia. If you break off one of its tiny branches, it will secrete a milky fluid, a charactistic of all members of the Euphorbia family. It is found all along the Atlantic seaboard from Quebec to Georgia, as well as around the Great Lakes.

COMMON SALTWORT

Salsola kali—GOOSEFOOT FAMILY. This is often a large, bushy plant, with stiff leaves that are barbed on the ends. Again, its flowers are very small and green. It is found on beaches from Newfoundland to Louisiana and blooms late in the summer. Sometimes it is called Russian Thistle, but actually this name refers to another species growing in the prairie region, *Salsola ten-ufolia*, which is considered an obnoxious weed.

SEA BLITE

Suaeda maritima—GOOSEFOOT FAMILY.   Similar to Saltwort but without the prickly leaves is the low-growing Sea Blite. It is branched but rarely grows over a foot in diameter. The pale-green leaves growing up the stem are quite fleshy and less than ½ inch wide. Its leaves are large compared to what we have been looking at: up to 6 inches long, heart-shaped and coarsely serrated. It can grow up to 6 feet tall, although most plants are shorter and spread over the sand. The flowers are small and inconspicuous, barely ⅛ inch in diameter, and again, grow out of the leaf junction. The fruits or seeds are 1 inch long and covered with hooked spines. The seed case contains two seeds in separate capsules, each ripening in successive years. It is found growing all along the Atlantic seaboard from Quebec to New Jersey and along inland pond and lake shores.

BEACH PEA

Lathyrus japonicus—BEAN FAMILY.   The beach often rises as it moves away from the water's edge, and here is where we will find this sprawling plant. It has compound leaves made up of six to twelve small, oval leaflets, smoky-green in color. The leaves end in tendrils which, if they can find a support, will climb up to 2 feet. A cluster of pealike flowers in shades of pink, blue, and lavender are found on a separate stem. The open seeds are like small peas. Some authorities say that they can be eaten, but since they are supposed to contain an alkaloid, they are considered poisonous. The Beach Pea blooms from midsummer into fall and is found on the shores from Maine to New Jersey and along the shores of the Great Lakes.

As the beach rises, dunes are created. The winds sweep and swirl the sands into interesting designs, often building dunes to

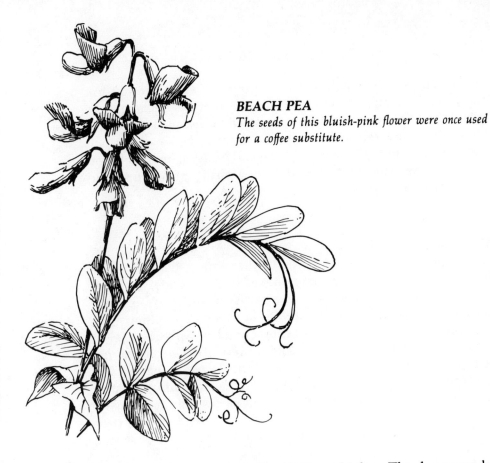

BEACH PEA
The seeds of this bluish-pink flower were once used
for a coffee substitute.

heights of 10 to 30 feet and sometimes higher. The dunes can be compared to the desert areas of Arizona.

BEACH PLUM

Prunus maritima—ROSE FAMILY. The beach plum is a straggly, woody shrub spreading its branches over the dunes. Its leaves are oblong, up to 1 inch, finely serrated, and alternate on the stem. The white, five-petaled flowers with multiple stamens are crowded on the stems, giving the appearance of a snowdrift on the dunes. It blooms in May and is found from Maine to New Jersey. The fruit makes a fine jelly.

DUSTY MILLER

Artemisia stelleriana—COMPOSITE FAMILY. We find this striking plant on the lee side of the dune. It is almost pure white. This is an adventive from Asia that was first introduced to gardens but escaped to the sandy areas and dunes where it has become quite established. It grows up to 2 feet. Its white leaves are about 2 inches long and serrated. Its yellow flowers are small, ¼ inch long, growing in tight clusters on the end of the stem. It is found all along the Atlantic seaboard from Canada to Virginia and along the Great Lakes.

WRINKLED ROSE

Rosa rugosa—ROSE FAMILY.   One of the shrubs that cannot be left out, the rose is a very common part of the seaside. It, too, is an alien from Asia, first used as a garden plant. It is a coarse, bushy plant up to 8 feet tall, with stout stems bristling with thorns. As with all roses, it has a compound leaf with up to seven leaflets, dark green and shiny. The flowers are 4 inches across with five lavender-pink, red, or, occasionally, white petals, and multiple yellow stamens. The bright-orange rose hips, about 1 inch in diameter, are used in the making of rose-hip tea or jelly. Considered high in vitamin C, rose hips are eaten by some people like little apples. I find them too full of seed for comfortable eating.

SEASIDE GOLDENROD

Solidago sempervirens—COMPOSITE FAMILY.   Scattered on both sides of the dune and beyond are found the showiest of the seaside plants, the Seaside Goldenrod. There is a species of goldenrod for just about every ecological situation in the United States; there are possibly 100 different species. This is distinctly an American genus. This tall, striking yellow-flowered plant can grow up to 6 feet tall on sturdy stems and is often found in groups. It has fleshy, smooth, green leaves. The flowers are found on the end of the stem, forming a brilliant yellow panicle. The individual flowers are ⅓ inch long. The showy variety is found from Canada to New Jersey, with a less spectacular form found farther south. Seaside Goldenrod blooms beginning in early September.

SEASIDE GOLDENROD
One of the few wildflowers that
can tolerate windblown salt spray.

PRICKLY PEAR

Opuntia compressa—CACTUS FAMILY.   We often think of cacti as part of the sandy deserts of western America, but they are also found in certain isolated areas on the dunes and in the sandy places from southern Massachusetts south. The Prickly Pear has fleshy, prickly, rounded leaves, with one growing out of the other, and terminally, a large, showy, yellow flower with numerous petals, sepals, and stamens. It grows close to the ground, forming a forbidding mat. Watch out if you should try to pick it as the prickly spines are quite troublesome.

JOINTWEED

Polygonella articulata—SMARTWEED FAMILY. This very dainty plant is found in sandy areas and dunes away from the water. It is about a foot tall with wiry, branching stems on which small threadlike leaves are found. Jointweed has tiny, bell-shaped flowers, white or pink. It grows from southwest Maine to North Carolina and along the Great Lakes. It blooms in late summer and in the fall, and it can be dried very nicely for use in dry bouquets.

BOGS

THE LEE SIDE OF THE dune, or the side away from the wind, is often steep and reaches down to a moist area where the wind has scoured out the sand and blown it up onto a higher dune on the opposite side. The dune behind the beach is called the primary dune; the higher dune on the opposite side is called the secondary dune. The depression in between is called a swale or bog. The floor of the swale or bog is moist, or even standing in fresh water. This, in turn, attracts a very different group of plants: those that grow in wet, acid places. This is a unique kind of landscape. Some bogs are the result of a dying pond; others are found along the edges of slow-moving streams. Most are covered with moss, primarily sphagnum; several species of moss carpet the floor. Let us seek out some of the exciting plants that are found in all kinds of bogs. Bogs display a parade of flowers that starts with the white Lance-leaved Violet in the spring.

LANCE-LEAVED VIOLET

Viola lanceolata—VIOLET FAMILY. Its white flower is typically violetlike in arrangement, with five equal petals. The lower ones are usually larger than the rest, spurred at the base, and veined with dull purple. The plant is from 3 to 5 inches high. The leaves growing from the base are long, narrow, and lance-shaped. Some authorities say that they are slightly fragrant.

BEACH HEATHER or FALSE HEATHER

Hudsonia tomentosa—ROCKROSE FAMILY. Often in these bogs you will see a mound of sand extending above the bog, covered with a gray-green, scalelike plant which hugs the mound. At the end of May there is an explosion of yellow flowers growing from the tips of its many branches. The flowers are five-petaled and only bloom in the bright sunshine. Beach Heath ranges from New Brunswick along the coast to North Carolina and also along the Great Lakes to Minnesota.

CRANBERRY

Vaccinium macrocarpon—HEATH FAMILY. This is perhaps the plant that is most at home in any bog. The flowers are pinkish, with four backward-pointing petals, each about ½ inch long. The stamens meet at a point. The leaves are about ⅔ inch long, oval, shiny on the top side but dusty underneath, and are evergreen, although in the winter they turn dark red. The creeping branches extend up to 10 inches and beyond. The flowers bloom from June to August and, in the fall, produce bright, sometimes dark, red fruits that are quite edible. Our cultivated species were originally derived from this wilding. They are found from Newfoundland to the North Carolina mountains, and west to Minnesota.

CRANBERRY

The fruit of this interesting flower is important commercially both as a jelly and juice. The original name for this plant was craneberry because its petals resembled a crane.

YELLOW-EYED GRASS

Xyris caroliniana—YELLOW-EYED GRASS FAMILY. Often growing among the Cranberry, this is a tall flower, up to 16 inches in height, with narrow, straplike leaves to 8 inches tall. The flower grows from a stalk that rises from a cluster of leaves at the base. An odd-looking plant, it has a three-petaled flower found at the top of an oval head of scalelike bracts not unlike a tiny pine cone. It ranges from Nova Scotia to Florida near the coast, and west to Michigan.

The wild orchid may perhaps be called the pièce de résistance of the bogs. Let's look at three different varieties that may be found growing there, but remember, *wild orchids should never be picked.*

ROSE POGONIA

Pogonia ophioglossoides—ORCHID FAMILY. Sometimes called Snake Mouth, this orchid, blooming late in June, is the first of the wild orchids to bloom. It sports the typical orchidlike flower, in a beautiful shade of pink, growing at the end of a slender stem. It is about 2 inches long with three petals and three sepals,

ROSE POGONIA
Sometimes this beautiful rose-colored plant is called by the ungraceful name of Snake Mouth.

all pink, and a spoon-shaped bract, fringed in yellow, at the bottom of the flower. It has a single leaf growing out of the flower stem. I have seen them growing en masse, but more often they are found growing in small groups. The Rose Pogonia grows in a wide range of wet areas from Newfoundland along the coast to Florida, and inland to Minnesota; it is also found in Indiana, Illinois, and Pennsylvania.

GRASS PINK

Calopogon pulchellus—ORCHID FAMILY. It is a beautiful pink color, with up to ten flowers growing in succession on a naked stem. There are three petals, with one long one extending upward covered with yellow, orange, and magenta hairs. It has three broad, spreading, pink sepals. It has one long, straplike leaf growing on the flower stem. It has the same geographic range as the Pink Pogonia.

LADIES' TRESSES

Spiranthes cernua—ORCHID FAMILY. This is a third orchid that blooms in this area in late August and in September. When you first see them, you will think that you have come upon a patch of late-blooming Lily-of-the-Valley. The white flowers are small, about ½ inch long. It is an orchidlike flower in design, with three fused sepals forming a head over the frilled lower lip. The flowers grow up a naked stem in a spiral fashion. The leaves are long and grasslike, growing from the base of the flower stem. Again, they are found in the same range as the Pink Pogonia and the *Calopogon*.

One of my students said recently that he heard a very strange thing: that there are plants that eat insects. I told him that it is true. There are two that are most often seen in the bogs of the Northeast.

PITCHER PLANT

Sarracenia purpurea—PITCHER PLANT FAMILY. It is a startling-looking plant, up to 20 inches tall, and is the largest of this type of plant to be found in this area. It has a basal rosette of tubular leaves from 4 to 12 inches tall. The top of the leaf is flared and scalloped; it is colored green, sometimes tinged with red. The inside of the leaf is covered with down-pointing hairs, so that when the insect is attracted to the sweetish nectar within the leaf and walks or flies in, it is trapped and drops to the bottom into a liquid composed of rainwater and digestive enzymes. The plants absorb the nitrogenous chemicals in the insect because the plant grows in soil that is poor in the nitrogen necessary for plant growth. The red flower is odd: it looks like an opened umbrella. As a matter of fact, it looks like two umbrellas looking at each other. The Pitcher Plant is apt to be rare in some areas, so do not pick it. Its geographic limits are wide—from Saskatchewan to Labrador, south through New England to Florida, west to Texas, and north to Minnesota.

SUNDEW

Drosera intermedia—SUNDEW FAMILY. It is a small plant, 4 to 9 inches tall. The sundew has a basal rosette of spreading leaves, each about ½ inch long, covered with granular hairs that secrete a sticky substance. A drop of this at the end of each hair glistens in the sunlight. Hence the name. The flower stem growing out of the basal rosette is about 4 inches tall, with several white flowers. They are small, with five petals growing terminally on the stem. When insects are attracted to the leaf, they are stuck as they alight; this plant is senitive to anything that hits the hairs. The hairs secrete a digestive enzyme and curl over the insect, again extracting needed nutrients from the insect. This plant has the same geographic range as the Pitcher Plant, and they often grow together. There are several other species, some of which are particular as to where they grow.

As the season advances, the other wildflowers in the bog begin to bloom.

PURPLE GERARDIA

Agalinis purpurea—SNAPDRAGON FAMILY. It has also been called *Gerardia purpurea*. It has a pink or purple-pink, bell-shaped

PURPLE GERARDIA

This dainty bell-shaped flower grows in wet places among the Ladies' Tresses that bloom at the same time, presenting an attractive picture.

flower, ¾ to 1½ inches long, that ends with rounded, flaring lobes. The flowers are found at the junction of the leaf and stem. The stem can be up to 4 inches long, but frequently it is much shorter. Its leaves are up to 1½ inches long and ½ inch wide and opposite on the stem. Purple Gerardia grows from southern Massachusetts across to Illinois, and south to Texas; it generally blooms from August through September.

BOG ASTER

Aster nemoralis—COMPOSITE FAMILY. Asters are daisylike flowers with disk flowers in the center, encircled by ray flowers. In the fall, asters literally cover the countryside, growing in most ecological situations. One of the many species is the Bog Aster. The ray flowers are a light purple and the disk flowers yellow, but it is considered a single flower. It grows terminally on the stem and is about 1 to 1½ inches across. The leaves are lancelike and numerous, growing up the stem and tapering at both ends; the leaves are directly attached to the stem. Bog Asters are found from Newfoundland to New Jersey, and west to Michigan.

THREAD-LEAVED GOLDENROD

Solidago microcephala—COMPOSITE FAMILY. Goldenrods are another ubiquitous group of flowers, with about 88 species—some say 100—in the United States, growing in all kinds of areas. Perhaps the daintiest of them all, the Thread-leaved Goldenrod is found growing in damp, sandy, open areas and bogs. Its leaves are less than ⅛ inch wide and about 1 inch long. The plant stands about 1 foot or more in height. The flowers are in tiny yellow clusters terminally on the stem. It is found from southern New England to Florida along the coast. Compare this with the Seaside Goldenrod.

CROSS-LEAVED MILKWORT

Polygala cruciata—MILKWORT FAMILY. Another resident of the damp bogs, some cling so close to the ground that you might step on it before you see it. Its flowers are found in a purple tuft on the end of the stem, which may be only 1 inch out of the ground. The leaves are narrow, lance-shaped, and arranged in fours around the stem. They bloom from July to September. Cross-leaved Milkwort is found from Maine to Florida, west to Texas, and north to Minnesota.

STAR-FLOWERED FALSE SOLOMON'S SEAL

Smilacina stellata—LILY FAMILY. This plant is often found in the sand that borders bogs. It stands 10 to 20 inches high. Its leaves are lanceolate and folded along the midvein, directly clasping the stem. They ascend up the stem. The white flowers are ¼ inch across, star-shaped, and found in clusters at the end of the stem. Blooming from May through August, it is found from Canada to New Jersey, and west to Minnesota.

PINEWEED

Hypericum gentianoides—St. Johnswort Family.   This is another interesting plant because of its size and location in the damp sand near the bogs. It is a bushy, wiry plant about 3 to 10 inches tall. Its leaves are almost scalelike, running up the stem. The single, five-petaled flowers are yellow, only ⅛ to ½ inch across, and are generally terminal on the stem. It blooms in the summer and the fall. Pineweed is found from Maine to Florida, and west to Texas.

SALT MARSHES

5

MOST RIVERS AND STREAMS EVENTUALLY lead to the open ocean. Many become wide bays and are subject to tides, just as the ocean is. Often their shores and inlets are shallow, due to a buildup of sediment, and form salt marshes that are subject to tides. It is here that a certain colony of grasses dwell, surviving in a salty situation because they have learned to cope with salt. As the tide runs out, the marsh is drained of seawater. At low tide, the grass closest to the water's edge is called Cord Grass (*Spartina alternifolia*), which sometimes grows to 8 feet tall and tolerates the greatest amount of seawater. Halfway up the marsh we find that the Salt Marsh Hay (*Spartina patens*) takes over. At the upper edges of the Salt Marsh Hay is a group of wildflowers that can abide growing at the edge of the high-tide line. We have alredy mentioned some, such as the Seaside Goldenrod, Sea Rocket, and *Atriplex*. Like the beach flowers, marsh flowers bloom in the summer and early fall.

MARSH ROSEMARY or SEA LAVENDER

Limonium nashii—LEADWORT FAMILY.   Dressing the upper marsh in a lovely mist of blue, this many-branched flower stem rises out of a whorl of lance-shaped leaves that narrow at the base. The plant ranges from 6 to 24 inches tall. The flowers are blue, about ⅛ inch across, and grow densely on branching stems. They are found in salt marshes from Newfoundland south. They dry nicely and can be used in dried arrangements.

MARSH ELDER

Iva frutescens—COMPOSITE FAMILY.   This plant will show you the dividing line between the marsh and the high ground. It is a coarse, woody plant with fleshy, serrated leaves and can reach a height of 10 inches. The tiny, greenish flowers are found intermingled with the leaves on the stem. It ranges from Nova Scotia south.

SWAMP ROSE MALLOW

Hibiscus palustris—MALLOW FAMILY.   This is the flower that really lights up the marsh. Growing at the edge of the salt marsh,

SWAMP ROSE MALLOW

The mucilaginous juice in the roots was once used as an ingredient in candy.

its large, rosy-pink, five-petaled, bell-shaped flowers look almost unreal. The flowers can be up to 7 inches in diameter. It is a tall plant, growing up to 8 feet. Its leaves are up to 4 inches long, yellow-green with a bloom on the undersides. They are oval, serrated, and come to a point. There is a similar plant often growing in the same area, with a white flower that has a red or purple center. It ranges from southern Rhode Island to Florida, and is also found around the Great Lakes.

SEASHORE MALLOW

Kosteletzkya virginica—MALLOW FAMILY. Farther south from Long Island to Florida and west to Louisiana on the edges of salt marshes or brackish marshes, we find this close cousin to the Swamp Rose Mallow. It has a smaller flower, ½ to 2½ inches wide, and pink petals. The leaves are oval and three-lobed with a velvety stem. The plant is about 2 to 4 feet high. The flowers are terminal, growing on a short stem. It blooms from May to October, depending on location.

SALT-MARSH ASTER

Aster tenuifolius—COMPOSITE FAMILY. This is one of the two species of asters found among the grasses in the upper reaches of the salt marsh. A perennial, it has a daisylike flower and is made up of two groups of flowerlets. The yellow disk flowers in the center are about 1 inch in diameter. Its leaves are fleshy, long, and narrow. It can reach a height of 2 feet but usually it is less. It is found from New Hampshire to Florida, and west to Mississippi. It blooms in late August and September.

ANNUAL SALT-MARSH ASTER
Aster subulatus—COMPOSITE FAMILY.   It is a small-flowering annual. Its many flowerheads are only about ½ inch across and are found on branching stems. The ray flowers are pink-purple and very short. The leaves are very narrow, lanceolate, and up to 6 inches long; the plant can grow up to 3 feet in height. It is found in coastal salt marshes along the Atlantic seaboard.

SEA PINK
Sabatia stellaris—GENTIAN FAMILY.   Tucked in among the salt marsh grass at the upper edge is this elusive and rare flower. It is delicately beautiful, pink with a yellow center. It has five widely-spaced petals, each about ¾ inch wide. The leaves are elliptical, narrowing at the base, and about ¾ to 1½ inches long. The Sea Pink can grow up to 3 feet in height. It ranges from southeastern Massachusetts to Florida.

SILVERWEED
Potentilla anserina—ROSE FAMILY.   This is an interesting plant growing in the salt marshes and along the wet shores. The flower is borne on a naked stem rising from runners. Being a member of the rose family, the yellow flower has five petals and is about 1 inch wide. The leaves are compound, with seven or more sharply serrated leaflets of a rich green, silvery underneath. The plants spread by means of runners. It blooms from May to September and is found from Long Island northward to Canada.

GLASSWORT or SAMPHIRE
Salicornia europaea—GOOSEFOOT FAMILY.   The striking thing in a salt marsh in the early fall are patches of bright-red Glasswort.

Upon closer inspection, we can see that it is a mass of individual plants made up of fleshy, jointed, green stems with no apparent leaves. The leaves have been reduced to scales. The flowers are very tiny, green, and grow out of the upper joints. Glasswort is found in salt marshes from Canada to Georgia and blooms in the middle of the summer. The stems of these plants can be pickled, or eaten raw; however, they are very salty.

SALT-MARSH FLEABANE

Pluchea purpurascens—COMPOSITE FAMILY. It is rather tall for a salt-marsh plant, growing up to 3 feet in height. Its flowerheads are made up of only disk flowers, pinkish purple, about ⅕ inch in diameter, all growing to the same height terminally on the stem, giving the plant a flat-topped look. This plant gives off a faint camphor fragrance. It leaves are up to 6 inches long, almost stalkless, ovate, and slightly toothed. Its range is from southern Maine to Florida, along the coast.

NARROW-LEAVED CATTAIL

Typha augustifolia—CATTAIL FAMILY. This is a flower of the brackish marshes along the coast, generally found on the high edge of the marsh. Looking at it, it is hard to believe that it is a flower at all. The flowers are found on dense spikes 4 to 8 inches tall. The male and female flowers are separate. At the top 5 inches of the spike, you will find the pollen-producing, or male, flowers; hundreds of little flowers compressed together. Below is a space of about 2 inches, and then the female flowers will be found in a dense, cylindrical cluster of dark brown. They actually bloom in June or July. The leaves are narrow and straplike, coming up from the root to a height of 5 feet or more.

There are a few wild flowers found in the cracks of rock ledges along the coast and in bay areas.

SEASIDE PLANTAIN

Plantago juncoides—PLANTAIN FAMILY. This probably won't strike you as a flower at all. However, its flower stem is 2 to 8 inches long, coming out of a basal rosette of narrow, fleshy leaves almost as long as the flower stem. The flowers are located terminally, crowded into a compact tuft of yellow stamens which are the most visible at blooming time. There is also a closely related species growing on sea beaches and salt marshes called *Plantago maritima*. They are found from Canada to New Jersey.

SCARLET PIMPERNEL

Anagallis arvensis—PRIMROSE FAMILY.   This is a low-growing or sprawling plant. The flowers have five petals about ¼ inch long and brick red in color, but sometimes they are blue and white. The flowers are found on the end of the stem that grows out of the junction of the leaf and the main stem. These flowers will open when the sun is out. The leaves are ¼ to 1¼ inches long, egg-shaped, and grow directly out of the main stem. This plant is an adventive from Europe. A word of caution: It may cause dermatitis, so be careful. It blooms from May to August, from Maine southward.

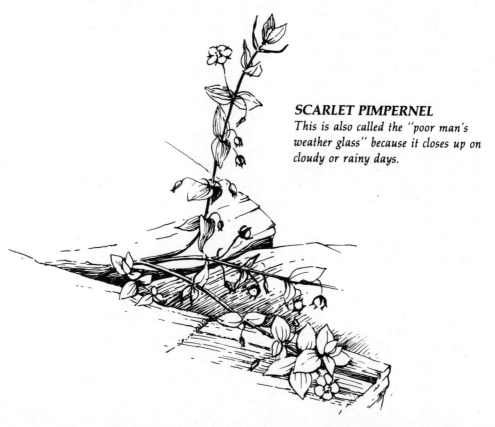

SCARLET PIMPERNEL
This is also called the "poor man's weather glass" because it closes up on cloudy or rainy days.

ROSEROOT

Sedum rosea—SEDUM FAMILY.   This is a succulent plant with an affinity for rocky cliffs. Its flowers are pinkish-purple and small, ¼ inch in diameter, growing terminally on numerous stalks. Its leaves are fleshy and oval, about 1 inch long, growing in a spiral up the stem. It grows from Maine to North Carolina.

YELLOW THISTLE

Cirsium horridulum—COMPOSITE FAMILY.   Another plant growing in dry meadows bordering the sea is this forbidding-looking plant. It is extremely bristly, so do not try to pick it. However, look at it carefully. The sepals and bracts under the flower are artistically beautiful. Its thistlelike flower looks like a yellow brush about 3 inches long. The leaves are deeply serrated and very thorny. It grows from Maine along the coast to Florida, and west to Texas; it blooms in the middle of the summer.

HORNED POPPY

Glaucium flavum—POPPY FAMILY.   This is another plant found blooming in waste places and on pebbly beaches in bay areas. It has found its way from Europe and is about 3 feet high with a single large, yellow flower growing terminally on the stem. Since it is in the poppy family, it has four petals. The leaves near the flower wrap themselves around the stem, but lower down they have a stem that joins the main stem. These are deeply lobed and are covered with a white bloom. When the flowers go to seed, they form a pod which is sickle-shaped and can range up to 12 inches in length. It blooms from June to August and is found from Massachusetts to Virginia.

These are some of the fascinating flowers you will find along or near the seashore as you walk the beach, the dunes, the bogs, the waste places, and the salt marshes.

WOODLANDS

Early Spring

MOVING AWAY FROM THE FRESH ocean breezes to the land, we find that there are many different ecological areas, each with its particular types of plants. However, some plants are so versatile in their requirements that they may grow in several different areas. Some are so particular in their requirements that they will be found only in special places. Land areas are broken up by lakes, ponds, rivers, bogs, marshes, swamps, mountains, fields, woodlands, rocky cliffs, as well as cities. Some of our so-called native plants were at one time brought from Europe or Asia on purpose or accidentally.

The acidity or alkalinity of soil also determines the plant growth. Oak forests are highly acid since oak trees contain tannic acid. Granite rocks are also acid, while limestone and marble present an alkali soil. Some clay soils are heavy and water resistant; other soils are sandy and porous.

Let us begin with the deciduous woodlands, where the first flowers of spring appear, before the canopy of the trees leaf out and the sun's warmth reaches the forest floor. The woodlands may be dry or they may be damp.

The woodlands are places where the wildflowers make their first showing, from early April to the middle of May. Most of the spring flowers are perennial and have been marking time underground, waiting for the sun's signals.

TRAILING ARBUTUS or MAYFLOWER

Epigaea repens—HEATH FAMILY.   This is one of the first to bloom. The name Mayflower has nothing to do with the month of May; actually the plant is named in honor of the boat that brought the Pilgrims to our shores. It is a trailing plant that keeps its leaves all winter. Its tiny flowering buds are formed the autumn before and huddle close to the ground, responding to the early spring sun even if the snow has not yet left. The fragrant flowers are ½ inch across, pink or white, tubular, with five pointed spreading lobes. The flowers grow in clusters and are generally found on banks. The leaves are oval, leathery, hairy along the edges, and up to 3 inches long. It can bloom as early as March, and is found from Newfoundland to Florida, and north to Kentucky and Iowa.

LIVERLEAF or HEPATICA

Hepatica americana—BUTTERCUP FAMILY. Like the arbutus, its buds remain under the leaves on the plant all winter, and with the warming days it blooms very early. It is not a perfect flower for it has no petals but six to eight colored sepals with numerous pistils and stamens in the center of the flower. The leaves are three-lobed, leathery, and sometimes bronze-green. These leaves fall off after blooming and a new set matures. The flowers cluster together and, along with the stem, are covered with fine hairs, a protection against errant weather. It ranges from southern Canada to Nova Scotia, south to Georgia, Tennessee, and Missouri. It gets its name, Liverleaf, from the shape of its leaves, and because of this it was once thought to cure liver ailments.

BLOODROOT

Sanguinaria canadensis—POPPY FAMILY. This plant is also an early riser, sending up a bare, smooth stem on the top of which is a pure white flower, 1½ inches wide, with eight to ten petals and a bright-yellow center of many stamens but only one pistil. The blue-green leaves emerge out of the ground, clasping the flower stem, and are lobed and scalloped. It grows up to 10 inches high and ranges across Canada to Nova Scotia, south to Florida, and west to Texas. Like most members of the poppy family, it exudes a fluid when the stem is broken, in this case, red. In times past, it had many uses both for dyes and medicines. It ranges from Canada to Florida, west to Texas, and north to Manitoba.

WOOD ANEMONE or WINDFLOWER

Anemone quinquefolia—BUTTERCUP FAMILY. Walking in the woods on an early spring day, you may come across a mass of these flowers, nodding their heads as the breeze catches them: hence the name. A single white flower grows on the end of a single stem, 4 to 8 inches high. Like the Hepatica, it does not have any petals, but rather white sepals and numerous pistils and stamens. Below the flower is a whorl of three segmented leaves, each made

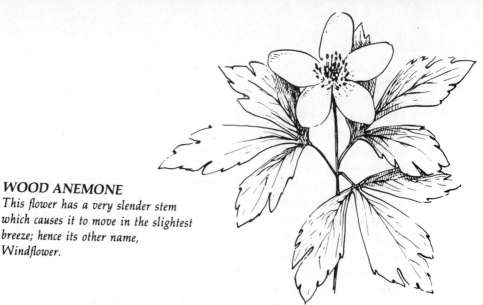

WOOD ANEMONE

This flower has a very slender stem which causes it to move in the slightest breeze; hence its other name, Windflower.

up of three to five leaflets with deeply serrated edges. It ranges from Quebec to western New York, south to North Carolina, and locally in Ohio and Kentucky.

TROUT LILY

Erythronium americanum—LILY FAMILY.   The Trout Lily is another early spring flower that grows in large masses in the damp woodlands. The flower is lilylike with three yellow petals, three yellow sepals, and six stamens with brownish or yellow pollen. The flowers grow singly on the top of the smooth stem. The petals and sepals are outwardly curved and grow up to 10 inches high. The spotted leaves are eliptical and long, growing out of the base of the flower stem. This flower has a very short growing period; it is completely gone by June. You cannot find the place where it grew. It is sometimes called Dogtooth Violet; however, it is no way related to the violet family.

COMMON BLUE VIOLET

Viola papilionacea—VIOLET FAMILY.   It has a typical violet flower, ½ to ¾ inch wide, with five petals. Two of the lateral petals are bearded. All the petals are strongly veined from the center of the flower. The leaves are heart-shaped with slightly serrated edges. The plant also has another flower which grows close to the ground and produces quantities of seeds but fails to open. Violets are high in vitamins A and C, and can be used in salads and even cooked. An elegant touch to a cake can be made by decorating the top of it with candied violets. It is found throughout.

Violets are a popular symbol of spring. There are about 800 species widely distributed around the world, and the woodlands are not without their share, brightening up the various corners.

BELLWORT

Uvularia sessilifolia—LILY FAMILY.   Sometimes called Wild Oats because the seed looks like the seed of oats. Like many spring flowers it is dainty, only about 6 to 10 inches tall. Its flowers are cream-colored, bell-shaped, and droop from the top of the stem. Its light-green oval leaves, up to 3 inches, are found at an angle out from the main stem. It ranges from New Brunswick and Nova Scotia to Georgia, west to Missouri, and north to North Dakota. Bellwort is apt to grow in masses, and when a forest breeze moves over them, it will set them all in motion.

PERFOLIATE BELLWORT

Uvularia perfoliata—LILY FAMILY.   A similar species, it is a single drooping flower with six petals of creamy yellow. The flower is found at the top of a sparsely leafed stem. The interesting thing about the plant is that the stem appears to grow through the leaf. The leaves are light green and about 3 inches long. It is found from Quebec to Florida, west to Louisiana, and north to Kentucky and Tennessee. It has an affinity for rich woods.

SOLOMON'S SEAL

Polygonatum biflorum—LILY FAMILY.   This is an interesting plant. It has a single, curved stem growing out of the ground. The leaves are stalkless, from 2 to 5 inches long, light green, and grow alternately up the stem. Small, drooping, six-petaled flowers, ½ to ¾ inches long, grow in pairs at the leaf junctions. The early colonials and the Indians used the roots as a source of starch. The leaf, when broken from the root, leaves a scar resembling the official seal of King Solomon. Solomon's Seal ranges from the northern United States to Georgia, and west to Kentucky.

FALSE SOLOMON'S SEAL

Similacina racemosa—LILY FAMILY. The white flowers of this plant are found terminally in pyramid-shaped, branched clusters. They are very tiny, ⅛ inch long, with six petals. The stems are 1 to 3 feet long and gracefully curved. The leaves are 3 to 6 inches long, oval, pointed, and grow up the stem. The fruit is a berry, but should be eaten with caution as they are a cathartic. These last four species are closely related and often grow together, with False Solomon's Seal blooming the latest.

CLINTONIA

Clintonia borealis—LILY FAMILY. This plant was named after De Witt Clinton, the former governor of New York. This is a plant of the cooler parts of our area. It has a basal rosette of large, oval, shiny leaves up to 8 inches long. Growing from this, on a separate bare stem, are terminal clusters of yellow flowers, each with six petals about ¾ inch long. In the fall it has bright-blue berries which give the plant the nickname of "blue bead." These berries are reputed to be poisonous, though some authorities dispute this. Clintonia ranges from Labrador through New England, south to the mountains of Georgia.

WHITE BANEBERRY

Actaea pachypoda—BUTTERCUP FAMILY. At the top of a tall, straight stem, 1 to 2 feet high, is a rounded group of feathery flowers. Each little flower, ¼ inch long, is white, with six to ten petals and many white stamens. Baneberry has compound leaves—usually three sharply toothed leaflets. It is sometimes called Doll's Eyes because its fruit is white with a black dot at the flower end and bright red stems. It ranges from Minnesota to Quebec, south to Georgia, and west to Louisiana and Oklahoma.

RED BANEBERRY

Actaea rubra—BUTTERCUP FAMILY. A closely related species, it is very similar to the above, except that the berries are bright red, and the species occurs much father north—Labrador and Newfoundland, south to New Jersey. The berries of both species are very poisonous.

SWEET WHITE VIOLET
Viola blanda—VIOLA FAMILY.   It is a pity that our American violets do not have the fragrance of the English violets. However, down in the rich woods there is a small, white violet that is sweetly fragrant. This flower is ½ inch wide, irregular, and five-petaled. The lowest petal is striped with purple. The upper petals curve upward. The leaf is rounded, heart-shaped, and indented where it joins the red stem. It ranges from Quebec to Minnesota, and south to the mountains of Georgia and South Carolina.

JACK-IN-THE-PULPIT
Arisaema triphyllum—ARUM FAMILY.   Now here is a plant that does not look like a flower. As a matter of fact, you cannot see its flowers because they are on a stem or spadix deep inside a cowl, with the male and female flowers separate. The cowl is like a leaf or bract and is called a spathe. It has a hood over the opening. Despite its sanctimonious name, it is death to the insects that crawl or fly in there and cannot climb up the slippery sides of the

JACK-IN-THE-PULPIT
Also called "Indian turnip." Although the Indians gathered the roots as a vegetable, they are somewhat hot and poisonous.

spathe. It is also called Indian Turnip because Indians used to boil and eat the roots as a vegetable, but these plants are poisonous when raw. It ranges from southern Quebec and New Brunswick through the Applachians, south on the coast to Florida, and west to eastern Texas.

WILD COLUMBINE

Aquilegia canadensis—BUTTERCUP FAMILY. One of the few red flowers in the Northeast. It is a drooping flower with five red petals extending into long tubes behind the flower, where the nectar collects. It is said that the hummingbirds do not come north until the Columbine blooms. There are numerous yellow stamens. The flowers are from 1 to 2 inches long. The leaves are large and compound, with three serrated leaflets. It can grow up to 2 feet tall, and has an affinity for rocky places growing out of the cracks in the boulders. It ranges from Ontario to Quebec, south through New England to Georgia, west to Tennessee, and north to Wisconsin.

Trilliums are a very attractive group of flowers. I will mention those that you would be most apt to see depending on the location of the forest. The one thing to remember about trilliums is that all parts of the plant are in threes.

NODDING TRILLIUM

Trillium cernuum—LILY FAMILY. Found in damp acid woods, it hides its flower under the leaves. It has three white, recurved petals about 1½ inches long. Above the flower is a whorl of three oval leaves. It ranges from Newfoundland and Nova Scotia through New England to Maryland, Delaware, and the mountains of Georgia and West Virginia.

LARGE FLOWERED TRILLIUM

Trillium grandiflorum—LILY FAMILY. The showiest, its flower is up to 4 inches across, white, turning pink as the plant ages. Like all other trilliums it has three petals, three sepals, and six stamens. Under the petals is a whorl of three leaves up to 6 inches long. The plant grows up to 18 inches tall. It is found in woods where the soil is basic or neutral. It is found from Ontario, Quebec, western Maine, and New Hampshire south to Georgia, west to Arkansas, and northward to Minnesota.

WAKE-ROBIN or BIRTHWORT

Trillium erecta—LILY FAMILY.   This trillium gets its names from several sources. Wake-robin refers to the time when the robins return. Birthwort or Birthroot refers to the fact that a concoction was made from the roots and was used in delivery. It was also used for snakebites and other ailments. It has a foul odor that attracts flies. Like all trilliums, Wake-robin has a single red flower at the end of the stem. The three petals are about 1½ inches long and spread outwardly. A whorl of three leaves 7 inches long are found below the flower. This wildflower ranges from southern Canada south through New England to Delaware, and in the mountains to Georgia, west to Tennessee, and north to Michigan. They vary in color from white to yellow and green.

PAINTED TRILLIUM

Trillium undulatum—LILY FAMILY.   This is the loveliest of all the trilliums. The three white petals are marked with a red line at the

PAINTED TRILLIUM
The most beautiful of all the trilliums because of the red veining in the white flower.

base. It is 2½ inches wide, and like the others, it has a whorl of pointed leaves just under the flower. It can grow up to 20 inches high and is often found under hemlock trees. It ranges from southern Canada through New England, to New Jersey and Pennsylvania, and in the mountains to Tennessee and Georgia.

CANADA MAYFLOWER

Maianthemum canadense—LILY FAMILY. A small flower that carpets the forest floor in the spring, it is fun for children to pick because it grows in large mats. The flowers are found on the end of a short stem about 4 to 6 inches tall. Canada Mayflower is a cluster of tiny, white flowers composed of two white petals, two white sepals, and four stamens. It is a traitor to its family because its parts are in twos instead of threes. The leaves are heart-shaped, and only two or three are found clasping the stem. It ranges from Manitoba to Labrador, south through New England to Pennsylvania and Delaware, and in the mountains south to Georgia.

WILD SARSAPARILLA

Aralia nudicaulis—GINSENG FAMILY. Like the Canada Mayflower, it is a ground cover, but it is much taller and blooms later. It is about 8 to 15 inches tall. The flowers and leaf stem come separately from the root. The flowers are terminal on a naked stem, in three rounded clusters of very tiny, green flowers. The leaves are compound, with three to five leaflets forming each of three leaves on the bare stem, and are found growing above the flowers. Its roots were once used in flavoring soft drinks. It ranges from Canada through New England, south to Georgia, and west to Colorado and Nebraska.

WILD GERANIUM

Geranium maculatum—GERANIUM FAMILY. A favorite path of mine through the woods is lined on both sides with this pinkish-rose flower that stands about 1 to 2 feet tall. Its flowers have five rounded petals, 1 inch long, growing in a loose cluster on the end of the stem. It leaves are five-parted and deeply serrated on the ends. It ranges from New England south to South Carolina, and north to North Dakota.

WILD GERANIUM
*All parts of this plant contain tannin,
long used as an astringent and for other
medical purposes.*

INDIAN CUCUMBER ROOT

Medeola virginiana—LILY FAMILY.   Here is an odd flower with an
odd name. It is a tall plant, up to 3 feet in height, growing in
masses, with one main stem coming from the root. At the top of
the stem are several flowers. They have three yellowish-green,
very narrow petals that are recurved. The sepals are also yellowish-green and recurved. The stamens are brick red. Just above
the flower is a whorl of three oblong leaves, 1 to 3 inches long,
which turn a beautiful shade of red in the fall. Halfway down the
stem is another whorl of from six to ten leaves. They are 2½ to 5
inches long, oval, with pointed tips. The name comes from the
white tuberlike rhizome, which has a delicate cucumber flavor
that was relished by the Indians. It ranges from Nova Scotia west
to Minnesota and south through New England to Virginia, Tennessee, and the mountains of Alabama.

GAYWINGS or FRINGED POLYGALA

Polygala paucifolia—MILKWORT FAMILY. Here is an unconventional flower. It looks like a tiny, rose-colored airplane and is often confused with native orchids. The petals are ¾ inch long and are rolled into a tube with a fringe on the lowest petal. Two of it five sepals extend laterally and are rose-colored. The leaves are about 1 inch long and are found in a group at the tip of the stem. The leaves are evergreen, but they fall off when the new ones leaf out in the spring. It ranges from New Brunswick across to Saskatchewan, south through New York to the mountains of Georgia. It is quite often found growing under conifers.

EARLY SAXIFRAGE

Saxifraga virginiensis—SAXIFRAGE FAMILY. Out of a tiny basal rosette of very small leaves which appear to come up very early, or are possibly formed the autumn before, arise tiny flowers in a compact cluster close to the ground. As the season advances you will see that the flowers are on a hairy stem that can extend to 16 inches. The flowers are ¼ inch wide with five petals. The leaves hugging close to the ground are up to 3 inches long and are scalloped. It is found from Canada through New England to Georgia, west to Missouri, and north to Minnesota. It name means "rock breaker" for it seems to be found in the cracks and crevices of boulders and rock outcroppings.

SPRING BEAUTY

Claytonia virginica—PURSLANE FAMILY. This is a plant whose flowers are in loose clusters at the end of the stem. They are white with a pink stripe, ½ to ¾ inch wide, with five petals and five stamens with pink pollen anthers. The leaves are 2 to 8 inches long, a single pair on the main stem about halfway up. It ranges from Canada through New England to Georgia, west to Texas, and north to Minnesota. Its roots are considered excellent eating. When boiled, they have the flavor of chestnuts.

These are some of the flowers that you will see in the rich and sometimes damp woodlands in April and May. Early spring woods are open and the spring flowers take advantage of the increasing sunlight. However, the wheels are being set in motion toward early summer and you will find fewer flowers because the woodlands will be closing into deep shade in some areas. Go look for the spring flowers and enjoy their beauty and you will find that life will take on a new dimension.

7

WOODLANDS

Midsummer

JUNE AND JULY ARE SOMETIMES the hottest months of the year. The flowers you find growing in the forest now are those that have adapted to shade or partial shade. Some grow along the immediate edge of the forest. The woodlands are cooler and damper than the surrounding open areas due to the photosynthesis, or food-making process, of the trees. The flowers of the forest floor share their space with other plants such as ferns and low-growing shrubs. It is a quiet and restful place, clothed in many shades of green and the dappled shadows of the forest floor.

PINK LADY'S SLIPPER

Cypripedium acaule—ORCHID FAMILY. The most spectacular flower of the early part of June is the Pink Lady's Slipper or Moccasin Flower. Here is an unconventional-looking plant, appearing like a balloon on the end of the stem. Upon further inspection, you will see that the pouch or balloon has a slit in the middle to allow for the entrance of the pollinators to their pollen and nectar. Actually it is two petals fused together. The third is a brown petal hanging down in back. To the side and above are three brown sepals. The flower stem rises directly out of the ground with two long, oval, 8-inch leaves at the base. The leaves are green above but silvery underneath. They are often found growing under oaks and pines in sandy soil, and occasionally they are found growing in damp areas. They range across Canada, south through New England to South Carolina and Georgia, west to Alabama and Tennessee, and north to Minnesota. Do not pick it or try to transplant it, because picking it kills the whole plant.

YELLOW LADY'S SLIPPER

Cypripedium calceolus—ORCHID FAMILY. Unlike the Pink Lady's Slipper, the yellow has its pouch on a leafy stem with two twisted, yellow-brown side petals. It has two sepals, greenish-yellow and lance-shaped, one located above the flower and one below. The flower is about 2 inches long. There are usually three to five leaves on the flower stem, oval, and coming to a point. The

YELLOW LADY'S SLIPPER
It derives its name from the Latin word for "little shoe."

veining in the leaves is parallel. It is found in rich woods, swamps, and bogs from Newfoundland to the mountains of Georgia, and west to Texas. It is found in less acid soil than the Pink Lady's Slipper. Do not pick it as it is becoming rare. It has hair on its foliage that can cause an allergic reaction.

WHORLED POGONIA

Isotria verticillata—ORCHID FAMILY. This is another orchid found growing in the acid woodlands. It is found in woods that are made up primarily of oak trees. Its small flowers are found singularly at the end of a 6- to 12-inch stem that has a whorl of five or six smooth leaves, each about 3 inches long. The flower is small, yellow-green, and orchidlike, with three slender, brown sepals, 1 to 2 inches long, extending beyond the flower. It is said it grows up from a marshy area. The Whorled Pogonia is rare. It ranges from Maine to Florida, west to Texas, and north to Wisconsin.

WHORLED LOOSESTRIFE

Lysimachia quadrifolia—PRIMROSE FAMILY. This flower is often seen in the woodlands and on the edges of woods at this time of the year. The interesting thing about this plant is that the leaves and flowers grow together in a whorl of four, five, or six along the main stem. The flower is yellow, with five petals, about ½ inch long, joined at the base; it has a red center with a red line running up the middle of each petal. The leaves are light green, 2 to 4 inches long, and ovate. There can be numerous whorls on one stem. It ranges from Ontario to Maine, through New England, south to Georgia, west to Alabama, and north to Illinois and Wisconsin.

BUNCHBERRY

Cornus canadensis—DOGWOOD FAMILY. It is rather an attractive flower, growing close to the ground and related to the dogwood tree. What looks like four white petals are actually four white bracts—colored leaves growing at the top of the stem. These surround the actual flowers. The flowers are a rounded cluster of tiny greenish flowerets. Underneath the flowerhead is a whorl of six broadly oval leaves, 1½ to 3 inches long. In the fall it has a cluster of bright berries which are edible, although insipid. In times

BUNCHBERRY
This small plant is a member of a family whose relatives are mostly trees and shrubs.

past it was used for various ailments, including paralysis, heart trouble, and even colic. It ranges across Canada to Labrador, south to Maryland, and west to South Dakota and Minnesota.

SHINLEAF

Pyrola elliptica—WINTERGREEN FAMILY. This plant was once used for bruises and wounds, hence the name. It is evergreen, with its rounded leaves seen in the snow. Its flowers are ¾ inch wide, white, bell-shaped, five-petaled with an extended pistil. The flowers are found in succession up a stem that is 6 to 10 inches in length. The leaves are found in a basal rosette. They are about 3 inches in diameter, growing on a stem about as long as the leaf. They are found across southern Canada through New England, and south to West Virginia.

COW WHEAT

Melampyrum lineare—SNAPDRAGON FAMILY. This is one of the few flowers on the forest floor in the middle of the summer. It is a low-growing, branching plant, 4 to 10 inches tall. The lower leaves are lanceolate, and the upper ones are somewhat toothed. The flowers are irregular, less than ½ inch long, opening into two lips with the lower lip three-lobed. They are straw-colored and are found singularly at the junction of the leaf and the stem. Cow Wheat ranges from southern Canada to New England, and south along the mountains to Georgia. It is parasitic. The Dutch at one time cultivated it to feed cattle—a possible explanation for the name.

PIPSISSEWA or PRINCE'S PINE

Chimaphila umbellata—WINTERGREEN FAMILY. This is a rather attractive woodland plant at this time of the year. It is 6 to 12 inches high and evergreen. Its flowers are small, pinkish-white, and found in a cluster at the end of the stem. They have five petals which are recurved and fragrant. The leaves are fleshy, slightly serrated, about 3 inches long, and arranged in several whorls up the stem. It is especially fond of dry sandy woods. It was earlier used by the medical profession. It does contain salicylates which are found in aspirin. It is found from southern Canada through New England to Virginia, and west to California.

SPOTTED WINTERGREEN

Chimaphila maculata—WINTERGREEN FAMILY. This is closely related to the above but grows in rich woods and flowers in midsummer. It is also evergreen. It has a single white or pink waxy flower at the end of a single stem about 9 inches high. The flower is about ¾ inch in diameter, five-petaled, and fragrant. The leaves grow in several whorls of three and are lanceolate, tapering to a point at the end. They are dark green with a white stripe following the rib. In the winter the underside of the leaf turns a dark red and can be seen above the snow. It is found from Ontario to North Carolina and South Carolina, and across to Alabama and Kentucky, especially in the mountain areas.

WOOD LILY

Lilium philadelphicum—LILY FAMILY. We tend to think of lilies as garden flowers. We have some beautiful species that grow wild, including this brilliant orange one. It grows from 1 to 3 feet tall with an upward-facing, bell-shaped flower with three orange petals and three orange sepals. The inside of the flower is flecked with brown dots. There are several whorls of five or more narrow leaves. There may be one to three flowers. They are found in thin, sunny woods from Maine to North Carolina, west to Missouri, and north to Minnesota.

NORTHERN FALSE FOXGLOVE

Aureolaria flava—SNAPDRAGON FAMILY. This plant has a spike of lemon-yellow, bell-shaped flowers. The flowers have five fused petals and sit close together on the stem. The leaves are lance-shaped, broad at the bottom, and covered with fine hairs. This plant is a parasite on the roots of oak trees. It ranges from Maine to Wisconsin, and south to Florida and Louisiana.

FERN-LEAVED FALSE FOXGLOVE

Aureolaria pedicularia—SNAPDRAGON FAMILY.   A very similar relative, it is very much like the above except that its leaves are deeply serrated and covered with fine hairs. It is also more bushy than the Smooth False Foxglove. Its range is similar to the above.

SPIDERWORT

Tradescantia virginiana—SPIDERWORT FAMILY. This flower is bright blue, with three rounded petals and yellow stamens growing in a cluster at the top of the stem. Its leaves are grasslike and extend beyond the flower. It is a wilding that is sometimes planted in gardens. It grows in open woods and is especially fond of roadsides. There is also a white variety. It ranges from Maine to Minnesota and south.

As you can see, there's much to observe in the midsummer woods.

WOODLANDS

Late Summer

S THE SEASON PROGRESSES, THE days become shorter. In August, and sometimes in September, the heat is still with us. If the summer has been hot and dry, the woods begin to look weary, as if waiting for a change. In September the nights can get frosty, putting an end to the growing period. However, in southern New England and southward, frost is fairly late and many of the summer flowers will continue to bloom. Even a few of the early spring flowers will bloom again when the days are shorter. There are some species of flowers that do not start their flowering until this time of year.

Various species of asters are blooming at this season. The asters are composites, daisylike flowers with two kinds of flowers: ray flowers, and disk flowers in the center. There are many species so that it is best to acquaint yourself with a few.

SMOOTH ASTER

Aster laevis—COMPOSITE FAMILY. It likes the dry woods and roadsides. The flowers are about 1 inch in diameter, a bluish-lavender color. The flowers are found singly on a short stem. The plant is 1 to 4 feet tall. The leaves are thick, slightly serrated, lanceolate, and 1 to 4 inches long, clinging directly to the main stem. The main stem is covered with a whitish bloom. It ranges from southern Ontario through New England, south to Georgia, west to Louisiana, and north to Kansas.

WHITE WOOD ASTER

Aster divaricatus—COMPOSITE FAMILY. This plant has a flat cluster of flowers about 1 inch wide growing terminally on the stem. The whole flowerlet is white; however, the disk flowers turn a bronze-purple as the flower ages. It stands 3 feet tall with large, heart-shaped leaves that are serrated and have long stems. It likes dry, open woods and roadsides. It ranges from northern New Hampshire to northern Georgia, west to eastern Alabama, and north to Ohio.

PURPLE ASTER

Aster patens—COMPOSITE FAMILY. This is a slender-stemmed aster. The ray flowers are bluish-violet, about 1 inch in diameter, and the yellow disk flowers are found individually on short stems at the end of the main stem. The plant is up to 3 feet tall with a rough and slender stem. The leaves are oblong and clasp the stem. It ranges from southern Maine and New Hampshire to Florida, west to Texas, and north to Missouri and Kansas. It has an affinity for dry woods.

BLUE-STEMMED GOLDENROD

Solidago caesia—COMPOSITE FAMILY. This is one of the few goldenrods that grow in the woods and is different in design. It stands 2 to 4 feet on a slender, blue stem. Its leaves are 3 to 5 inches long; small clusters of flowers grow out of the junction of the leaf and stem, crowding near the top of the stem. Because of its weak stem, the plant is often found bent over. It ranges from southern Canada through New England to Florida, west to Texas, and north to Wisconsin.

SILVERROD

Solidago bicolor—COMPOSITE FAMILY. Here is a goldenrod that is not golden. Its flowers are white: both the tiny ray and disk flowers. The flowers are found in clusters on short stems near the top of the main stem. It is from 1 to 3 feet tall with oblong basal leaves up to 4 inches long, but the leaves gradually get smaller as they go up the stem. It likes dry woods. It is found from southern Canada to Georgia, west to Arkansas, and north to Wisconsin.

INDIAN PIPE

Montropa uniflora—INDIAN PIPE FAMILY. Scattered throughout the woods at this time of the year are groups of dead-white plants with no green on them at all. The Indian Pipe is called a saprophytic plant because it cannot make its own food and gets it from decaying plant material. The ½- to 1-inch, five-petaled

INDIAN PIPE

Although this plant looks very much like a fungus, it is a true flowering plant.

flower droops singularly on the end of the stem. It has white scales up the stem but no leaves. It grows to about 6 inches tall. Because of its color, it was once thought to be related to mushrooms and therefore edible, but it is not. It is, however, a true flower and more closely related to the rhododendron. It ranges from southern Canada across the United States in rich woods.

RATTLESNAKE PLANTAIN

Goodyera pubescens—ORCHID FAMILY. The leaves are more attractive than the flower. The flowers grow on a single stem rising from a basal rosette of interesting leaves. They are oval in shape, green overlaid with a network of white lines. The flower found near the top of the stem is actually a series of small, globular flowers. It ranges from southern Canada through New England

RATTLESNAKE PLANTAIN

This member of the orchid family has leaves that resemble the skin of a snake. It was once thought to be a cure for snakebites.

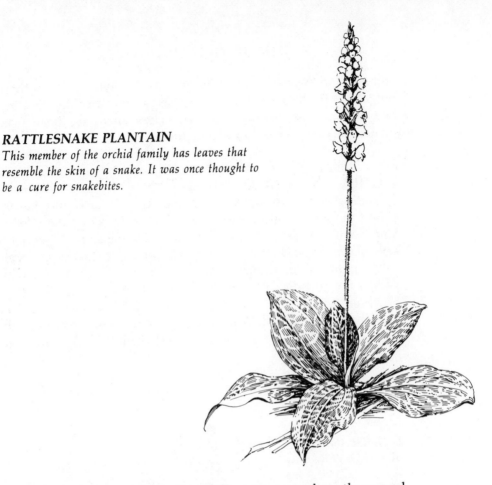

to Florida, west to Arkansas and Tennessee, and north around the Great Lakes. Because the design of the leaf resembles the skin of a snake, it was once thought to be a cure for snakebites.

WINTERGREEN

Gaultheria procumbens—HEATH FAMILY.   Creeping over the sandy forest floor is a woody, vinelike plant with glossy evergreen leaves, 1 to 2 inches long. If you crush a leaf you will find that it has a strong wintergreen odor. It is also called Teaberry or Checkerberry. The flowers are found in clusters on upright stems growing from prostrate stems. They are bell-shaped, with five fused petals. Wintergreen has an affinity for oak and pine forests. It ranges from eastern Canada to Georgia, west to Alabama, and north to Wisconsin and Minnesota. However, at its southern range it is in the mountains. The leaves are refreshing to chew and lend themselves nicely to tea. They also have been used medicinally, especially for rheumatism.

WOODLAND SUNFLOWER

Helianthus strumosus—COMPOSITE FAMILY. You would hardly expect to find a sunflower growing in the woods, but the Woodland Sunflower does. It is a tall plant, growing up to 7 feet, with several flowers at the top of the main stem. The flowers are typically sunflower in design, 2½ to 3½ inches in diameter, with yellow ray and disk flowers. The flowers surrounding the disk, however, are sparse. The leaves are 3 to 8 inches long and broadly lance-shaped, rough above and hairy underneath. It ranges from Maine to Florida, west to Texas, and north to Minnesota.

WOODLAND SUNFLOWER

We tend to think of sunflowers as plants that love the sun, but this one is at home in the woodlands.

WHITE LETTUCE or RATTLESNAKE ROOT

Prenanthes alba—COMPOSITE FAMILY.   This is a tall plant, growing to 5 feet. Its stem is smooth and purplish, with white or pinkish flowers in groups up the stem. The flowers, although composite, have only ray flowers about ½ inch long with prominent stamens. The leaves are large and variable in shape. They may be smooth or deeply serrated on the edges. It was once thought to be a cure for snakebite, because of its snakelike root. It ranges from southern Canada to Virginia, and north to North Dakota.

BEECHDROPS

Epifagus virginiana—BROOMRAPE FAMILY.   This is a parasitic plant. It gets its nutrients from the roots of beech trees. Since it does not make its own food, it has no green parts. It is a fleshy-tan in color, many-branched, with scales running up the branches. The flower is ½ inch long, tubular and flaring, with five lobes, two up and three down. The flower is also striped with purple. It is found wherever beech trees grow: southern Canada to northern Florida, and north to Wisconsin.

The growing period for woodland flowers more or less ends with the end of September. However, some may keep blooming until the frost. This is the time to look for dry grass and seed heads for dried arrangements.

WETLANDS

Spring

THE SMELL AND SOUNDS OF spring are in the air, and it is time to look for the first flowers of the season in the meadows and wetlands. Here is where the parade will start—in March, April, and May. Most of the wet places are the results of melting snows, spring rains, springs, and flooding. The water will stand in pools and may dry out but leave the ground damp. The trees have not yet leafed out, so the beneficial rays of the sun reach the floor, prodding the buds into bloom. Most of the flowers that grow here are perennials that have dormant buds.

SKUNK CABBAGE

Symplocarpus foetidus—ARUM FAMILY. The very first plant to show itself is the skunk cabbage, very aptly named as you will find out if you decide to pick a bouquet. Here is a plant that just can't wait for spring to come. It often starts to send up its bud as early as October and can even grow through the ice and snow. One year it bloomed in February because of the warm weather. The flowers are very tiny with no petals and no sepals, and are found on a yellow club deep inside a cowl, a leathery bract or colored leaf of red, yellow, or green, wrapped around the flowers to protect them from the cold. The leaves come up after the flower blooms and are very large—from 1 to 2 feet long—and literally carpet the wetlands. Scientists tell us that when the flower does come in bloom, it generates heat to protect itself, and also as an enticement for early carrion flies, which do the pollinating. It grows over much of southern Canada and the northeastern United States, south to the uplands and Georgia, and west to Iowa.

MARSH MARIGOLD

Caltha palustris—BUTTERCUP FAMILY. Another early wetlands plant but far more attractive than Skunk Cabbage is the Marsh Marigold or Cowslip, a golden-yellow flower. It has no petals, only sepals that turn from green to bright yellow. The flowers are from 1 to 1½ inches in diameter, with multiple yellow stamens characteristic of the buttercup family. It is 1 to 2 feet high and has dark-green, kidney-shaped leaves, 2 to 5 inches wide. It ranges from Canada through New England to the mountains of North Carolina and Tennessee, and west to Iowa. It was once used as a pot herb, but the raw plant is very poisonous, and if you must eat it, it must be cooked in three changes of water to leach out the poisonous glucoside.

EARLY MEADOW RUE

Thalictrum dioicum—BUTTERCUP FAMILY. The Early Meadow Rue is a tall plant, up to 30 inches high, but the interesting feature of this plant is that the male and female flowers are on separate plants. The male plant is quite showy: it has no petals or sepals, only clusters of greenish-white stamens, about ¼ inch long, hanging in groups like tassels. The female plant has only small, elongated purple pistils. It has compound leaves reminiscent of Maidenhair Fern. It ranges from southern Canada to Georgia, west to Missouri, and north to Minnesota.

FALSE HELLEBORE

Veratrum viride—LILY FAMILY. False Hellebore is a tall, coarse plant, growing to 7 feet. Its leaves are large, 6 to 12 inches long, parallel veined, and seem to grow directly out of the stem. The flowers, on the other hand, are very tiny, with three petals and three sepals growing tightly on branching clusters at the end of the stem. This plant comes up very early in the spring, but it also dies out early in the summer. Its roots and leaves are very poisonous. It is said that when the Indians were about to choose a new chief, the candidates were fed this plant, and the one that survived became the new leader. It is found from southern Canada through New England to Maryland, in the uplands to Georgia and Tennessee, and north to Minnesota.

GOLDEN RAGWORT

Senecio aureus—COMPOSITE FAMILY. This plant is 1 to 2 feet tall, smooth stemmed, and topped with flat clusters of daisylike flowers. The disk and the ray flowers are both yellow. Its upper leaves are deeply serrated, while the basal leaves are heart-shaped. Wet places are its home. Its woolly seed head is said to look like an old man, hence its generic name, which means "old man." It ranges from southern Canada through New England to South Carolina, west to Missouri, and north to North Dakota.

COLTSFOOT

Tussilago farfara—COMPOSITE FAMILY. This plant was brought from Europe, possibly because it was used medicinally for coughs and allied diseases. It has a single dandelionlike flower, 1 inch in diameter, and stands from 3 to 18 inches tall. The flower comes up before the leaves, which are rounded in the shape of a colt's foot. It is found growing in wet places and streamsides. It ranges from Newfoundland, Nova Scotia, and New England to New Jersey, west to Ohio, and occasionally as far west as Minnesota.

CELANDINE

Chelidonium majus—POPPY FAMILY. Celandine was originally imported from Europe, possibly because it was used for medicines and dyes. The plant exudes a yellow fluid when the stem is broken, and this was used for dyes. It was also thought to be good for liver problems. The flower has four bright-yellow petals, ¾ inch in diameter, growing in a cluster at the end of the stem. The leaves are a soft-green, from 4 to 8 inches long, and divided into lobes. This plant is poisonous and probably caused a lot of trouble. It ranges from southern Canada through New England to Georgia, and west to Missouri and Iowa. It favors wet and moist ground.

SPICEBUSH or BENZOIN

Lindera benzoin—LAUREL FAMILY. This is not a wildflower as such, but a shrub that lights up the wet places in the early spring. It has many branches and is about 15 feet high, with a cluster of tiny yellow flowers found at the nodes where leaves were located the previous year. The flowers emerge before the leaves and look like little round balls, ⅛ inch long, sepals and petals looking alike. The male and female flowers are found on separate bushes. The leaves are smooth, with no serrations, and aromatic. Its dried leaves can be used for a tea. It ranges from southern Maine to Virginia, west to Kentucky and Missouri, and north to Michigan, and is sometimes found in the mountains of Georgia.

SWAMP SAXIFRAGE
Saxifraga pensylvanica—SAXIFRAGE FAMILY. Unlike the Early Saxifrage that grows on rocks, this one grows in swamps. It does not live up to its name of "rock breaker." The flowers are located terminally on a hairy stem, up to 3 feet tall, that grows out of a basal rosette of large, lanceolate leaves. The flowers are ⅙ inch wide with five petals, greenish-white, and grow in clusters on short stems near the top. It ranges from Maine to North Carolina, and west to Missouri.

GOLDEN ALEXANDERS
Zizia aurea—PARSLEY FAMILY. This is a flat-topped yellow flower, growing terminally on a 1- to 3-foot stem. Actually, the flower is made up of tiny flowerlets. The leaves are compound, made up of three to seven serrated pointed leaflets that are 1 inch long. It has an affinity for wet places. It ranges from Saskatchewan and New Brunswick to Georgia, and west to Texas and Missouri.

SWEET WHITE VIOLET
Viola blanda—VIOLET FAMILY. This blooms early in the spring in wet places. It is a small, white violet with the typical violet flower: five petals, two erect, two lateral, and the fifth drooping in the middle. It has parallel purple lines running up to the center of the petal. The plant is 1 to 5 inches high. Its leaves are rounded, heart-shaped, and rather small in a basal rosette. It has small, self-pollinating flowers found at the base of the plant. It also has a slight fragrance. It ranges from Labrador across Canada and south in cool wetlands.

10

WETLANDS

Midsummer

THE TREES HAVE NOT YET completely leafed out, and the world is a panorama of shades of green. The wet places, marshes, swamps, and streamsides are still wet, some permanently so, while others may dry out as the summer becomes hotter. It is here we find an array of flowers that like their feet wet.

BLUE FLAG

Iris versicolor—IRIS FAMILY. The blue flag is an interesting flower. Since it is a monocot, it has three petals and three sepals. The three petals are long, narrow, and grow upward. The three sepals are broader, blue, and turn downward. The flowers are up to 4 inches in diameter. The leaves are long and straplike, growing at the base of a rather stout flower stem. The leaves are about 1 inch wide and 32 inches long. It ranges across Canada through New England to Virginia, west to Ohio, and north to Minnesota.

BLUE FLAG

This beautiful flower was the emblem chosen by King Louis VII of France.

SLENDER BLUE FLAG
Iris prismatica—IRIS FAMILY.   A closely related species, it is very similar to the Blue Flag except that the leaves are very narrow—⅛ to ¼ inch wide—and about 1 to 3 feet long. The flower is the same design and about 3 inches across. It has an affinity for marshes near the East Coast from Maine to Georgia.

TALL MEADOW RUE
Thalictrum polygamum—BUTTERCUP FAMILY.   It is an ethereal-looking plant. It is 2 to 8 feet tall, with a cluster of white, wispy flowers at the top of the stem. The flowers do not have petals, only white sepals that fall very early in the plant's blooming period. Male and female flowers are on separate plants. The male has many white, threadlike stamens, growing erect. The female plant may have one or more pistils and a few stamens. It has compound leaves made up of three roundish leaflets. It ranges from Ontario to Nova Scotia through New England to Georgia, and west to Tennessee and Indiana.

COW PARSNIP
Heracleum lanatum—PARSLEY FAMILY.   It is a tall, coarse-looking plant that can grow to 10 feet tall. The white flowers are terminal, in flat-topped clusters made up of many small flowers about ½ inch wide. The leaf is very large—from 3 to 6 inches across—with three lobes deeply serrated. In times past, this plant was used in many forms of medicine. Some authorities say the early shoots can be used as food and eaten raw in salads. The early Indians used it as a source of salt. It grows from Canada through New England to the mountains of Georgia, and west to Kansas.

WATER HEMLOCK or SPOTTED COWBANE
Cicuta maculata—PARSLEY FAMILY.   This is a tall plant and should not be confused with Cow Parsnip, for it is highly poisonous. The flowers are white and appear in a loose, dome-shaped cluster. The individual flowers are ⅙ inch in diameter. The leaves are

compound, long, narrow, and serrated. The main stem is streaked with red. It ranges from southern Canada through New England to Maryland and the mountains of North Carolina, and west to Missouri.

JEWELWEED

Impatiens capensis—TOUCH-ME-NOT FAMILY. This bright yellow-orange flower spotted with brown has a distinctive shape. It has a flaring cone ending in a downward spur. The cone opens out to a wide lobe. The flowers are found dangling on thin stems on short branches toward the top of the plant. The leaves are almost translucent, oblong, and 1½ to 3½ inches long. If the leaves are submerged in water, they take on a jewel-like appearance. If you crush the stem, a clear fluid oozes out which is useful in counteracting poison ivy, should you touch it. It has also been used for fungus diseases of the feet; scientists have confirmed that the plant has a fungacidal quality. The seeds ripen into long capsules which explode when touched, and the seeds are widely scattered. It ranges from southern Canada through New England to Georgia, and west to Oklahoma.

MONKEY FLOWER

Mimulus ringens—SNAPDRAGON FAMILY. Someone with a lot of imagination felt that the flower resembled the face of a monkey.

MONKEY FLOWER
Someone with a lot of imagination saw a monkey's face in this flower.

It is an irregular flower about 1 inch long. It has two lips: the upper one two-lobed, and the lower one three-lobed. The flower is lavender and sometimes pink, but rarely white. The stem is up to 3 feet high and square. The leaves are from 2 to 4 inches long, pale green, lanceolate, and clasp the stem. It ranges from southern Canada through New England to Georgia and North Carolina, west to Oklahoma, and north to Minnesota.

MEADOW BEAUTY or DEER GRASS

Rhexia virginica—MEADOW BEAUTY FAMILY.   This attractive purple-pink flower loves wet sand and is often found along pond shores. It has four almost square-looking petals with eight prominent stamens extending beyond the petals, giving the flower a resemblance to deer's antlers. The flowers are found on the ends of branching stems. The leaves are 1 to 2½ inches long, oval, and pointed and serrated; they grow directly out of the stem. Meadow Beauty is found from southern Canada to Florida, and west to Mississippi.

COLICROOT

Aletris farinosa—LILY FAMILY.   As its name implies, it was once used as a cure for colic. It is a tall spike, 1 to 3 feet in height, growing out of a basal rosette of straplike leaves, 2 to 7 inches long. The flowers are tiny—¼ to ½ inches long—white, and tubular. They crowd up the stem. It ranges from southern Maine to Florida, west to Texas, and north to Minnesota.

BUR REED

Sparganium americanum—BUR REED FAMILY.   This is an interesting plant. It grows up to 3 feet tall with a zig-zaggy stem. At intervals on this stem are white, globular flower heads, 1 inch in diameter, with male flowers higher on the stem than the female flowers. The leaves are straplike, up to 3 feet long, and up to 4¼ inches wide. It grows on shallow, muddy shores and is found throughout the whole eastern United States. Its seeds are food for muskrats, water fowl, and marsh birds.

BUR REED

This plant is of value to wildlife. The seeds are eaten by waterfowl and marsh birds, while the muskrat feeds on the whole plant.

The wetlands are home to many orchids, all very beautiful: Purple Fringed Orchid, Ragged Fringed Orchid, Arathusa, and White Fringed Orchid, to name some. Since this book is about the commonest flowers, we will only review one of these beauties.

WHITE FRINGED ORCHID

Habenaria blephariglottis—ORCHID FAMILY.   This member of the orchid family is attractive, with rather interesting individual flowers. The white orchidlike flowers, 1½ inches long, have a deeply fringed lower petal and a long spur, curved outwardly.

They are found growing around the stem, toward the top. The leaves are long and straplike, up to 8 inches long and ¾ inch wide. It ranges from Newfoundland to Virginia, and along the coastal plain to Florida and Mississippi.

MARSH ST. JOHNSWORT

Hypericum virginicum—ST. JOHNSWORT FAMILY. It differs from most of the St. Johnswort flowers, being pink instead of yellow. It has an affinity for wet places, especially streamsides and pond shores, where it tends to take over. The flowers have five petals, and cluster terminally at the end of a small stem that grows out from the junction of the leaf and the main stem. The leaves are oblong, rounded at the ends, and directly joined to the stem. The stems are up to 2 feet tall and weak, often sprawling along the ground. It is found from coastal Nova Scotia to New England, and south to Florida; it is also found around the Great Lakes.

WHITE SWAMP AZALEA

Rhododendron viscosum—HEATH FAMILY. The fragrance of the White Swamp Azalea on a summer's evening in July adds to the delight of a walk. The White Swamp Azalea is sometimes called Swamp Honeysuckle because of its fragrance, but it is in no way related to the honeysuckle. It is a shrub because of its woody stems. Its lovely white flowers, 1½ to 2 inches wide, are vase-shaped, with five pointed lobes that recurve. The pistil extends beyond the flower. The leaves are 1½ to 2½ inches long, oval, shiny on top, but hairy underneath. The flower is also covered with sticky hairs. It reaches up to 8 feet but is often much shorter. It ranges from Maine to Georgia, and west to Texas.

SHEEP LAUREL or LAMBKILL

Kalmia angustifolia—HEATH FAMILY. This is a small evergreen shrub. Its flower are a bright reddish-pink, cup-shaped, found in clusters midway up the stem. The stamens are turned back into the flower, but pop out when they are touched. The flower is only ½ inch wide. The leaves are lanceolate, dull green, and pale underneath. Its foliage is considered poisonous to livestock. It ranges from Canada through New England to Georgia, and northwest to Michigan.

TURK'S-CAP LILY

Lilium superbum—LILY FAMILY.   For sheer height the Turk's-cap Lily probably takes first prize. I have seen them 10 feet tall. The individual flowers are 2½ inches long, with three orange petals and three petal-like sepals. The petals and sepals are recurved and spotted with brown dots. The six stamens extend beyond the flower and have dark-brown dangling pollen anthers. The leaves are smooth, lanceolate, and whorled around the stem. They are found from New Hampshire to Georgia and Alabama.

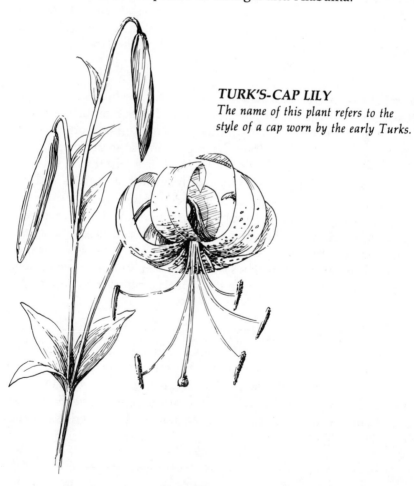

TURK'S-CAP LILY
The name of this plant refers to the style of a cap worn by the early Turks.

CANADA LILY

Lilium canadense—LILY FAMILY.   This beautiful lily is shorter than the Turk's-cap Lily, growing only to 5 feet. Its yellow to orange, brown-spotted flowers are bell-shaped, and droop downward on the stem. It has three sepals and three petals, 2 to 3 inches long, similarly colored. Many are often borne on a single plant, either at the junction of the leaf and stem, or at the end of the stalk. The leaves are 4 to 6 inches long, lanceolate, and found in a whorl around the stem. At one time the plant was served for food by the Indians. The flower buds were cooked and prepared like green beans. The bulbs were eaten. It ranges from Quebec to Maine, south to Alabama, and west to Ohio and Indiana.

HAREBELL

Campanula rotundifolia—BLUEBELL FAMILY.   This dainty flower is worth searching for in damp meadows, banks, or slopes. The Harebell is a bluebell-shaped flower, 1 inch long, growing singularly or in groups on wandlike stems. The flower has five lobes and lavender stamens. It leaves are 3 inches long, and narrow. There is another leaf at the base which is round, but it disappears before the flowers come into bloom. The plant can grow up to 20 inches in height. It ranges from northern Canada through New England to New Jersey, and from Indiana to Iowa.

11

WETLANDS

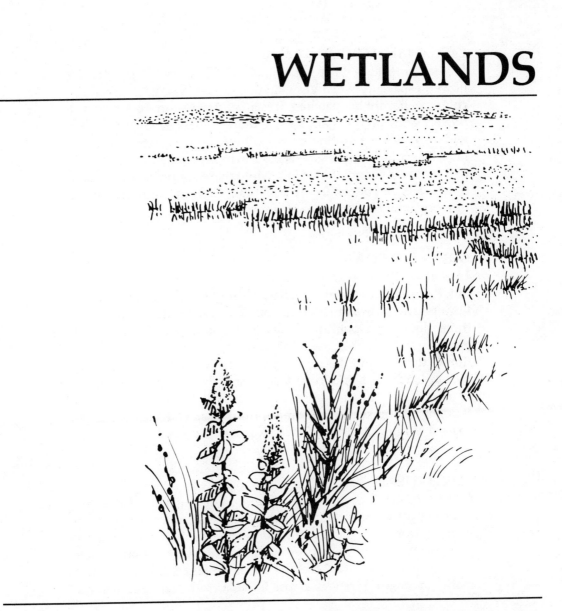

Late Summer

J ULY GIVES WAY TO AUGUST, but the heat of the summer still remains. The days are getting shorter, a dim reminder of fall. There are still many wildflowers to be seen, some of which are pretty spectacular.

CARDINAL FLOWER

Lobelia cardinalis—BLUEBELL FAMILY. This is a spectacular flower, especially when growing in a large mass. Its brilliant red color can hardly be matched. It is a tall flower—up to 4 feet. The flowers grow up the main stem and are 1½ inches long, tubelike, with three lobes pointing down and two pointing upward. It is a favorite of the hummingbirds. Its leaves are long and narrow, up to 6 inches in length. Once in a while there are mutations, where the flowers will be white or pink. It ranges from southern Canada to Florida, and west to Texas, and north.

GREAT LOBELIA

Lobelia siphilitica—BLUEBELL FAMILY. A counterpart of the Cardinal Flower, the Great Lobelia has bright-blue rather than red flowers, and grows in less acid soil. The flowers are tubular with three downward-pointing lobes and two upward-pointing. It grows up to 4 feet tall, with the flowers growing out of the junction of the leaf and the stem. The leaves are up to 6 inches long, oval or lanceolate, and irregularly serrated. Although the species name is unfortunate for such a beautiful flower, it was once thought to cure syphilis. It ranges from western New England to eastern Virginia, west to eastern Kansas, and north.

TURTLEHEAD

Chelone glabra—SNAPDRAGON FAMILY. The Turtlehead is an interesting plant with a flower that closely resembles its name. Its white flower is 1½ inches long, tubular, with the lower lip arching downward. The flowers grow in a terminal cluster on a single stem, which may reach 3 feet. Its leaves are lanceolate and up to 6 inches in length. It ranges across Canada from Newfoundland to

Minnesota, and south to Georgia and Alabama. Like its name-sake, it has an affinity for wet places.

NEW YORK IRONWEED

Veronia noveboracensis—COMPOSITE FAMILY. This is another beautiful tall flower of the wetlands. Its tall, straight stems end in a number of short stems, each bearing a cluster of purple flow-ers. The individual flowers are disk flowers; the ray flowers are absent. The leaves are up to 8 inches long, finely serrated, lan-ceolate, and end in a point. Its name refers to the stems, which are extremely tough and considered a scourge by farmers. It is found from Massachusetts and New York to Georgia, and west to Mississippi.

SWAMP ROSE MALLOW

Hibiscus palustris—MALLOW FAMILY. Here is another of fall's brilliant flowers, the Swamp Rose Mallow. The individual flow-ers are a rosy-pink, up to 6 or 7 inches across. It has five petals. The multiple stamens unite in a column growing out of the cen-ter of the flower. The leaves are more or less rounded and come to a point. They are light green in color with a whitish bloom underneath and are 4 inches long. The plant stands up to 8 feet tall. The flowers grow on short stems from the main stem. They are often found in large colonies and are a spectacular sight. They range from coastal Massachusetts to Florida, and around the Great Lakes Region.

JOE-PYE-WEED

Eupatorium maculatum—COMPOSITE FAMILY. This is a tall, rug-ged plant with dense terminal clusters of reddish-purple flowers, up to 6 inches wide. Its lanceolate leaves are coarsely serrated and whorl around the stem. This plant was used by an Indian named Joe Pye, who used it as a medicine for curing typhus. It ranges from Canada through New England to Maryland, Ohio, and Illinois.

JOE-PYE-WEED
Named for an Indian who first showed the colonists the medical uses of the plant's root as a cure for typhus.

BONESET

Eupatorium perfoliatum—COMPOSITE FAMILY. Boneset seems like a funny name to give to a plant. The leaves join each other at the stem, looking as if the stem pierces them, and because of this, boneset was thought to be good for application on bone breaks. The flowers are a dirty-white, in dense clusters at the end of the stem. The individual flowers are ¼-inch ray flowers. The leaves are lanceolate and coarse, with hair on the undersides. It ranges all over the eastern United States and as far west as Nebraska. Its height depends on where it grows and can be up to 6 feet.

CLIMBING BONESET

Mikania scandens—COMPOSITE FAMILY. This is a vine, and in places it can be insidious. The flowerheads, pink or white, are in branching flat clusters, and the individual disk flowerlets are ¼ inch wide. The stem can reach over 20 feet. The leaves are up to 3 inches long and are heart-shaped, sometimes with a serrated margin. It ranges from southern Ontario through New England to Florida, and west to Texas.

VIRGIN'S BOWER

Clematis virginiana—BUTTERCUP FAMILY. This is another vine of the wet places, which blooms late in the summer. Its white flowers grow in clusters out of the junction of the leaf and stem. The individual flowers lack petals; instead, the sepals serve as petals, with male and female flowers on separate plants. The male flowers have many flowering stamens, giving the plant a feathery look. The leaves are compound with three leaflets that are broadly oval, and pointed. Its trailing stems are up to 10 feet long. It ranges from Canada through New England to Georgia and west to Louisiana.

LANCE-LEAVED GOLDENROD

Solidago graminifolia—COMPOSITE FAMILY. Most goldenrods grow in dry places. However, there are a few that prefer damp soil. The Lance-leaved Goldenrod is one. It is a slender plant that branches out above the middle of the main stem. At the end of each branch is a tiny cluster of flowers with both ray and disk flowers. The leaves are almost threadlike, pointed, and up to 5 inches long. It can grow up to 5 feet, and can be found from southern Canada through New England, south to Alabama and possibly Florida, west to New Mexico, and north.

NEW ENGLAND ASTER

Aster novae-angliae—COMPOSITE FAMILY. You know it is fall when the meadows and swamps are ablaze with the pink and purple of the New England Aster. It is a tall plant, up to 7 feet in height, with a hairy stem. The daisylike flowers are ½ inch across. The ray flowers run from pink to purple. The disk flowers are yellow. The leaves grow thickly up the stem and clasp the stem directly, almost wrapping themselves around it. It ranges from southern Canada through New England to Maryland, west to Arkansas and New Mexico, and north to Wyoming.

NEW YORK ASTER

Aster novi-belgii—COMPOSITE FAMILY.   It is closely related to the New England Aster and sometimes confused with it. Its stems are smooth. It branches widely toward the top of the stem. Its flowers are ½ inch wide, with lavender ray flowers and yellow disk flowers, and are found on the end of the branches. Its leaves are lanceolate and quite narrow, joined directly to the stem. The whole plant is about 4 feet high and is found in Canada, Newfoundland, and Nova Scotia through New England to Georgia, primarily near the coast.

NODDING LADIES' TRESSES

Spranthes curnua—ORCHID FAMILY.   The tiny, white, orchidlike flowers, ½ inch long, are arranged in a spiral on a stem that grows out of a basal rosette of straplike leaves up to 10 inches long. The

NODDING LADIES' TRESSES
The individual flowers arch downward as if they are nodding.

flowers are nodding, quite fragrant, and grow in damp open places. It ranges from southern Canada through New England to Florida and Texas.

FRINGED GENTIAN

Gentiana crinita—GENTIAN FAMILY.   This is probably the most beautiful blue wildflower you will ever see, if you can find it. It is becoming increasingly scarce, due to destruction of its habitat. The flowers are about 2 inches long, bell-shaped with flaring lobes, growing singularly at the end of a parallel-branching stem. It blooms only when the sun is out; even a passing cloud can close it up. Its leaves are 1 to 2 inches long, lanceolate, but rounded at the base. It is found from Maine through New England to Pennsylvania, and west to Iowa. It is also found in Ontario. It loves damp places and streamsides.

CLOSED GENTIAN or BOTTLE GENTIAN

Gentiana andrewsii—GENTIAN FAMILY.   This is an odd-looking plant. The flowers are deep blue, budlike, 1 to 1½ inches long. The petals are only slightly separate, revealing a whole fringe. The flowers cluster at the top of the stem, with a whorl of 4-inch lanceolate or oval leaves just below the flower. This is found from Vermont and Massachusetts south to Georgia, and west to Arkansas.

GROUNDNUT

Apios americana—PEA FAMILY.   This flower is highly fragrant, almost cloyingly sweet. At its roots are edible tubers, which were a source of starch for the American Indian. The flowers grow in clusters at the end of a short stem. The main stem is a vine, about 10 inches long, that trails over other plants for support. The flower is pealike, with the bottom petals fused and recurving back to the flower. The leaves are oval and lance-shaped. It is found in wet places and moist thickets. It ranges from southern Canada through New England to Florida, west to Texas, and north to Minnesota.

JERUSALEM ARTICHOKE

Helianthus tuberosus—COMPOSITE FAMILY. This is a very tall, stout flower, 3 inches in diameter and sunflowerlike in design, with bright-yellow ray and disk flowers. The leaves are large, up to 10 inches long, very thick and sandpapery. They are broad at the bottom and come to a point. At the roots there are tubers which contain carbohydrates, but no starch. These edible tubers were particularly relished by the American Indian and as a matter of fact, were cultivated by them. It grows all across the United States, but it is an adventive in the East.

We have explored some of the flowers that bloom from early spring to late fall. Again, it depends on how early or late the frost comes. Fall is highly variable depending on your location, but by and large, most of the flowers have a definite blooming period.

12

PONDS AND BROOKS

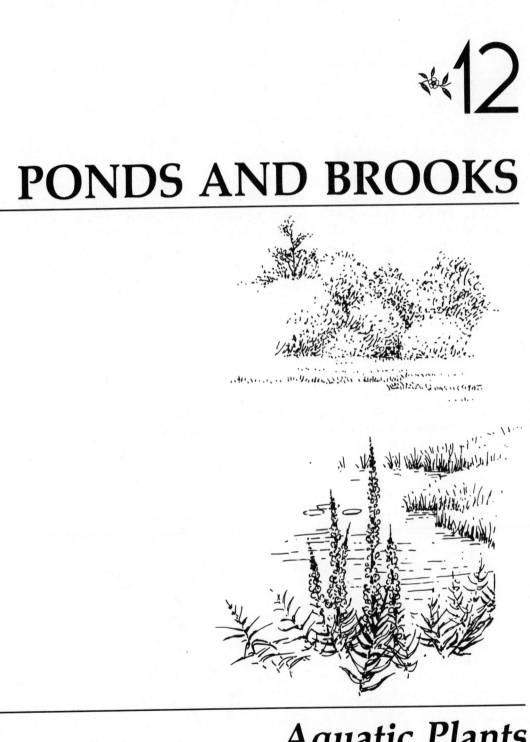

Aquatic Plants

THERE ARE FLOWERS THAT MUST grow in fresh water and these are the ones that we will explore now. In April and May the land plants, or those growing in damp places, bloom earlier than those that grow in water.

BOGBEAN or BUCKBEAN

Menyanthes trifoliata—GENTIAN FAMILY. One of the first to bloom, it is in no way related to the bean family. The flower is white with five petals each ½ to ¾ inch across with a bloom of white fuzz. The individual flowers are clustered at the top of the stem. The leaves are compound, with three leaflets, and are found on a stem rising out of the water. It ranges from northern Canada through New England to New Jersey and Virginia, west to Missouri, and then north. It has an affinity for cold-water swamps and marshes.

WILD CALLA LILY

Calla palustris—ARUM FAMILY. This blooms about the same time and in the same kind of a habitat. This flower comes out of the water among large heart-shaped leaves, which are up to 6 inches long and on a long stem. The actual flowers are very tiny, crowded together on a 1-inch stem, or spadix, and wrapped in a

WILD CALLA LILY

This beautiful flower yielded its roots to cooking in times past and was made into a flour for bread and cookies.

white spathe, which is actually a colored leaf that is curled and 2 inches long. The leaves are shiny and leathery looking. It ranges from southeastern Canada through New England to Pennsylvania, west to Indiana, and north to Minnesota.

GOLDEN CLUB
Orontium aquaticum—ARUM FAMILY.   This interesting plant grows in shallow water. The flowers are minute and perfect, with petals, stamens, and pistils. They are yellow, and crowded on a bare stem about 1 to 2 feet in length. The leaves are long, blade-like, and elliptical, up to 12 inches. The plant rises to 2 feet above the water and grows in colonies. It is found from Massachusetts through Florida, mostly along the coastal plain, and west to Mississippi and Kentucky.

ARROWHEAD
Sagittaria latifolia—WATER PLANTAIN FAMILY.   The flowers are found on a tall spike rising out of a basal rosette of large, strongly veined, shiny leaves. Like an arrowhead, the leaves are long, with two sharp, long lobes at the bottom of the leaf. The

ARROWHEAD
Once called "duck potatoes," it was a source of starch for Lewis and Clark on their trek across the country.

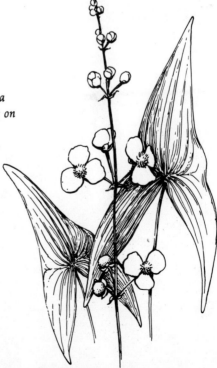

flowers are in a whorl of three around the top of the stem. They are white, with three sepals and three petals. The upper flowers are male with yellow stamens, and the lower flowers, where the seeds are found, are female. The Indians used to roast these seeds for food, often breaking open caches in muskrat lodges. It is found throughout the area.

PICKERELWEED

Pontederia cordata—PICKERELWEED FAMILY. This flower grows out of shallow fresh water. It is a tall plant with a spike of numerous tiny lavender-blue flowers at the top. They are bell-shaped, ⅓ inch long, with six lobes—the three upper ones joined and the three bottom ones separated. The leaves are heart-shaped to arrow-shaped. It ranges from southern Canada to Florida, west to Missouri, and north to Minnesota. It grows in large colonies, choking out other aquatic plants.

PICKERELWEED
Its starchy, nutlike seeds may be used as a cereal.

WATER PLANTAIN

Alisma plantago, aquatica, or *Alisma triviale*—WATER PLANTAIN FAMILY. This plant is found in muddy or shallow waters, swamps, or along stream edges. It is tall, 1 to 3 feet high. The main stem grows out of a whorl of elliptical leaves, sometimes heart-shaped. The main stem is symmetrically branched, with small-petaled, ¼-inch-wide flowers at the end of the branches. The root is edible and was used for food by the Indians. It ranges from southern Canada through New York, and west to Michigan, California, and Oregon.

WATER PLANTAIN

Alisma subcordatum—WATER PLANTAIN FAMILY. Very similar to the above; however, the leaves are narrower. The flower stems are less spreading, and the flowers are smaller, about ³⁄₁₆ inch long. It is found in shallow fresh waters from Vermont south to Florida, and north and west to Minnesota.

FLOATING HEART

Nymphoides cordata—GENTIAN FAMILY. It is hard to think of a member of the gentian family looking like a water lily, but the leaves do. The leaves are heart-shaped, from 2 to 8 inches in diameter, and float on the top of the water. From below the leaf, a cluster of white five-petaled flowers, ½ to ¾ inch wide, rises out of the water. It ranges from Newfoundland through South Carolina to Louisiana, along the coastal plain.

WATER LILY

Nymphaea odorata—WATER LILY FAMILY. A pond full of Water Lilies is a beautiful sight, but it also has an ominous ring. It means that the pond will soon be completely stagnant and will no longer be there. This plant is totally aquatic. Its shiny broad leaves, 4 to 10 inches in diameter, float on the surface of the water. The underside of the leaf is purple. The flowers are creamy white cups that rest on the water, and are 3 to 5 inches in diameter. They are made up of many petals, numerous stamens, and four green sepals. There is also a pink variety. The flowers are open from sunrise to noon. This plant was a source of food for the Indians. The long, oval flower buds as well as the roots were cooked and eaten. The flowers are very fragrant. It ranges throughout the whole country.

YELLOW POND LILY or SPATTERDOCK

Nuphar variegatum—WATER LILY FAMILY.   The Yellow Pond Lily often grows with the white one, but it does not have the beauty of the white. Its leaves are longer and more elongated, 6 to 10 inches long and broadly veined, radiating from the main stem that runs up from the bottom of the pond and reaches out of the water. The flowers have six bright-yellow petals and numerous stamens. It is cup-shaped, 1½ to 2 inches wide, with six green sepals. The flower reaches out of the water, not floating on it as the white flower does. They also signify a dying pond. The roots served as a source of starch for the Indians. It ranges across Canada south through New England, Delaware, and Maryland, and west to Iowa and Nebraska.

FEATHERFOIL

Hottonia inflata—PRIMROSE FAMILY.   The Featherfoil is another nonconformist. The leaves radiate out horizontally from an inflated stem and rest on top of the water. The leaves are finely toothed, 2½ inches long. The stem is jointed, and clustered around the joint and at the end of the stem are tiny ¼-inch, white flowers. It has an affinity for slow, sluggish waters which are less than 3 feet deep. It ranges from Maine to Florida, west to Texas, and north.

PIPEWORT

Eriocaulon septangulare—PIPEWORT FAMILY.   This tiny powder-pufflike flower often grows in masses on shores of shallow ponds. Its leaves are grasslike and submerged. The flowers are found singularly on a bare stem rising out of a basal rosette of leaves. The flowers are tight tufts of tiny white flowers, 1/16 inch long. The flowerhead measures ½ inch in diameter. It is found from southern Canada to Maryland and Virginia, west to Indiana, and north to Minnesota.

COMMON BLADDERWORT

Utricularia vulgaris—BLADDERWORT FAMILY. This odd plant grows only in water and has no visible leaves as such. The yellow, irregular flower is similar to a snapdragon, growing in clusters at the top of a bare stem 6 to 12 inches high. The stem is attached to branched, underwater stems by many very fine, threadlike leaves and tiny pulsating bladders attached to the leaves. These attract microscopic animals, who enter the bladders and are digested by the plant. Bladderwort is found in quiet, fresh waters from Newfoundland and Alaska, south to Florida and Texas, and west to Colorado.

WATER LOBELIA

Lobelia dortmanna—LOBELIA FAMILY. This member of the lobelia family grows in the shallows of ponds. It is a tall, smooth spike, up to 18 inches long. The blue flower is loosely spaced along the stem. It has five petals, with the two lower ones drooping. It grows out of a whorl of tubular leaves in the water. It ranges from Newfoundland south through New England to New Jersey, and west to Minnesota.

PURPLE BLADDERWORT

Utricularia purpurea—BLADDERWORT FAMILY. This is possibly the last flowering aquatic plant of the season in the northeast. It is much like the Common Bladderwort in design, but its stem is only 6 inches tall with only a single lavender-purple flower at the top. It has tiny, threadlike leaves with tiny bladders at the ends, used for capturing its food. It is found in quiet waters from Quebec southward along the coastal plain to Florida, west to Louisiana, and north to Minnesota.

13

OPEN FIELDS

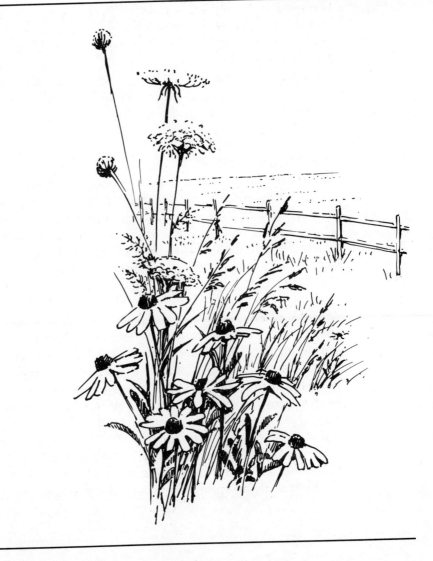

OPEN FIELDS, ALTHOUGH NOT A part of the original landscape of the eastern United States, were a product of man and his farming. But as farming decreases so do the fields, and they are now reverting back to woodlands, in natural succession.

An open field in the middle of the summer is a beautiful place as the wind ripples across the tall grasses. Interspersed in the grasses are many wildflowers. Some, as a matter of fact many, are immigrants from the western prairies and even from other countries.

Some field flowers are found along fences or stone walls and spill over to the roadsides. There are those that have an affinity for sloping banks. The soil in fields ranges from rich to poor, especially if sheep have been grazing. Field flowers are more adaptable than many other flowers. Like seashore plants, many bloom in the summer and the fall.

WHITLOW GRASS

Draba verna—MUSTARD FAMILY. Possibly the first to bloom, this plant grows in sterile areas, both on roadsides and in fields. It is barely 2 to 3 inches tall. Its tiny, white four-petaled flowers grow at the end of a stem which rises from a basal rosette of leaves about 1 inch across. They are so small they can be easily stepped on, so step lightly. It ranges from Massachusetts south.

DANDELION

Taraxacum officinale—COMPOSITE FAMILY. This next flower that spring produces in grassy places is considered a scourge on the landscape. Actually, it is a whole group of flowers forming a compact head at the end of a hollow stem, 6 inches or more in height, growing from a basal rosette of long, deeply serrated leaves. In times past, the dandelion had many uses and still does today, from wines made from the blossoms to coffee substitutes made from the dried roots. They can bloom around the calendar if there is no frost, but they do not seem too happy far south. Nothing lights up spring like a field of dandelions. When they go to seed, they form a fragile globe of seeds which disappears with a puff of wind. The dandelion came from Europe and Asia. It is said that the seeds can live twenty-eight days in salt water, so they can be carried to many distant places.

CYPRESS SPURGE

Euphorbia cyparissias—EUPHORBIA FAMILY.   Another early spring bloomer, it is related to the poinsettia. If you break the stem it will ooze a milky secretion, a mark of the Euphorbia family. It is an odd plant. Its stems are from 5 to 12 inches tall with many fine leaves running up and down the stem. At the end of the stem is an odd cluster of small flowers embedded in a cluster of yellow-green bracts. It ranges from Maine to Virginia, and west to Colorado. It is also an alien.

RED CLOVER

Trifolium pratense—PEA FAMILY.   This blooms in the spring but may continue on into late summer. A European plant, it was originally imported as food for cattle, but escaped. Its leaves are in threes, and are gray-green. The individual red flowers are pealike, and grow in a group at the end of the main stem and the branching stems. The flowers are about 1 inch long. Its height varies from 6 inches to 2 feet. In times past, the red clover had many medicinal uses which the medical profession takes a dim view of today. Of course, the four-leafed clover has always been a symbol of good luck.

BLUETS

Houstonia caerulea—BEDSTRAW FAMILY.   Beginning in April these tiny, dainty flowers are found in large masses—almost like drifts of bluish snow—or in small groups. They are found along roadsides and in open fields and lawns. The four flat petals, ½ inch wide, grow at the end of stems 3 to 6 inches long, which rise from a basal rosette of leaves ½ inch long. They bloom from April to June, and range from Nova Scotia to Georgia, west to Alabama, and north to Wisconsin.

PUSSY TOES

Antennaria neglecta—COMPOSITE FAMILY. Its flower suggests its name. It has very compact groups of furry, white flowers terminally on a stem which rises from a basal rosette of dusty-green leaves, oval shaped, ½ to 1 inch long. It is found in open fields, roadsides, and lawns from Ontario to Nova Scotia, south to Virginia, west to Indiana, and north to Minnesota. It is in the composite family, which includes dandelions, sunflowers, and daisies.

COMMON BLUE VIOLET

Viola papilonacea—VIOLET FAMILY. Again, as its name suggests, it is the one most often seen in fields, at roadsides, and on the edge of lawns. Violets, in varying shades of color, have five petals. The three lower ones are white at the base, and two of these are beautifully bearded. The flower is found at the end of a stem growing out of a cluster of deep-green, smooth, heart-shaped leaves. They are found all over the United States. A flower also grows near the root that fails to open and is self-pollinating, producing quantities of seeds. Sad to say, these violets have no odor; as a matter of fact, most of the North American species have no fragrance.

COMMON WINTER CRESS

Barbarea vulgaris—MUSTARD FAMILY. The Common Winter Cress makes quite a display in April in a field reverting back from cultivation. The flowers are small, ⅓ inch wide, with four petals forming a cross. They are bright yellow and are found on many branched stems growing out of a basal rosette of segmented leaves with a large and rounded terminal lobe. It is found from Ontario to Nova Scotia, south to Virginia, and west to Kansas. The young leaves may be cooked as a green or used raw in a salad. This is an introduced species, perhaps brought to our shores by Pilgrim ships.

14

FIELD FLOWERS

Early Summer

SO FAR, WE HAVE BEEN looking at the very early field flowers, which are very few compared with woodland flowers, one area we have explored. In May the summer pageantry of field flowers begins. Field flowers are generally taller than woodland flowers and have a longer growing period. However, some are low-growing.

COMMON CINQUEFOIL

Potentilla simplex—ROSE FAMILY.   The flowers grow out of the junction of the leaf and stem of this ground creeper. They are five-petaled, bright yellow, ½ inch wide, and look like tiny wild roses. The leaves are made up of five leaflets. It is generally found on sterile soil in fields and roadsides. Blooming from April to June, it ranges from Nova Scotia to Alabama, and west to Minnesota.

WILD STRAWBERRY

Fragaria virginiana—ROSE FAMILY.   This resembles the Cinquefoil. The flowers have five white petals, with several flowers on a stem growing from a basal leaf. Its leaves are made up of three leaflets. It, too, crawls over the ground. Though smaller, the red strawberries are much sweeter than the cultivated ones. It ranges throughout the area.

WILD STRAWBERRY
Its fruit is highly rated. Roger Williams praised its virtues in his statement that the "chiefest of Doctors of England was wont to say that God could have made but never did make a better berry."

BIRDFOOT VIOLET
Viola pedata—VIOLET FAMILY.   It is found growing along sandy roadsides and sandy fields. Its flowers are violet in color, about 1½ inches wide, larger than most of the violet family. It has five petals, with a whitish vein on the bottom petal. There is also a bicolored form, with its upper petals a deep purple and the three lower ones a lighter shade. Its leaves are palmate and deeply serrated. It ranges from Maine to Florida, and west to Texas. In the south it blooms early, and in New England it blooms in May.

TALL BUTTERCUP
Ranunculus acris—BUTTERCUP FAMILY.   There are more than thirty-three species of buttercups in our area but the one we remember best from our childhood is this species. It is common everywhere in open areas. It is especially fond of wet meadows. Its flowers are 1 inch across, a lustrous gold on the inside and lighter on the outside, with five overlapping petals with multiple stamens. The flowers are found at the end of long, slender stems. The leaves are deeply cleft, with three to seven divisions. It ranges throughout the area.

WHITE CLOVER
Trifolium repens—PEA FAMILY.   Another clover associated with an early May day, it grows by means of runners on the ground. The flowers and leaves grow separately from these runners. The flowers are compact heads of pealike flowers, white and sometimes soft-pink. The leaves are oval and three-parted with a faint triangular pattern on them. It grows in fields and roadsides and is found throughout the United States and Canada. It also came from Europe.

ALSIKE CLOVER
Trifolium hybridum—PEA FAMILY.   It is similar to the White Clover, though its habit of growth is different. The leaves grow from branching stems and do not have the triangular markings. Its

leaves are oval and in threes. Its flowers, like the White Clover's, are pinkish-white, in tight clusters of pealike flowers. It is found all over in fields, on roadsides, and in gardens. It, too, is an alien.

RABBIT-FOOT CLOVER
Trifolium arvense—PEA FAMILY. It is furry, with grayish-pink, compact flower heads. Its leaflets are narrow and covered with silky hairs. It grows in sterile fields and on roadsides and is common everywhere. It blooms from May to autumn.

RABBIT-FOOT CLOVER
Dried specimens make an interesting addition to dried arrangements.

BUTTER-AND-EGGS
Linaria vulgaris—SNAPDRAGON FAMILY. Introduced from Europe because it was thought to have medicinal properties, it is so called because of its two shades of yellow. Two-lipped with long

spurs, the flowers grow in a terminating cluster. The flowers are about 1 inch long, and the plant grows up to 12 inches high. Its leaves are very narrow, gray-green, 1 to 2 inches long, almost grasslike, growing tightly together on the stem. It is found in dry fields and waste places throughout the whole area. It blooms from May to September and even later.

ROBIN'S PLANTAIN

Erigeron pulchellus—COMPOSITE FAMILY.   Late in May, you may come across a patch of what looks like small pink daisies. Single flowers, sometimes two or three, grow terminally on a hairy stem rising from a basal rosette of elongated leaves that are widest at the ends. A few leaves are also found on the stems. The flowers are from 1 to 2 inches in diameter, with ray petals that are almost threadlike encircling yellow disk flowers. They are found from Maine to Georgia, and west to east Texas, and bloom from May into the early summer.

DAISY FLEABANE

Erigeron annuus—COMPOSITE FAMILY.   Its flower is pinkish to white, ½ to ¾ inch in diameter, with numerous flowers on the end of the stem. Like the Robin's Plantain, a close cousin, it has threadlike ray flowers around a yellow disk. It stands 1 foot or more. The leaves and stem are hairy, and the leaves are ellipitical in shape. Again, they bloom from late spring to fall. Considered a weed, it is an introduced species and is found all over the United States. It was once thought to be a good pesticide, hence the name.

COMMON CHICKWEED

Stellaria media—PINK FAMILY.   There are many species of chick-weed or stitchwort, but this one is the first to bloom. It is a weak-stemmed plant, about 16 inches tall, and has many branches. The white flowers have five ¼-inch-wide petals that are terminal on the branches. The leaves are narrow, green, ½ to 1 inch long. It grows in masses and can be a problem in a garden if it takes hold. It is found throughout.

15

FIELD FLOWERS

Midsummer—June

JUNE TREATS US TO THE longest days of the year and some of the best weather. Long, brilliant hours of sunlight with a shower now and then give the field flowers the best growing conditions. They have no need to hurry. Field flowers are often tall and have to compete with grasses.

DAISY or OXEYE DAISY

Chrysanthemum leucanthemum—COMPOSITE FAMILY. This is the first flower that comes to mind in June. It is not fussy, growing in open fields, meadows, pastures, and roadsides. It sometimes grows in large drifts, not unlike snow. It originally came from Europe, maybe because someone wanted a touch of home. The flower familiar to most of us is actually composed of two flowers, found singularly on the stem. The flower head has a compact center of yellow flowers with a collar of white ray flowers. Its green leaves are coarsely serrated, running alternately up to the flower head, and attached directly to the stem. It is found throughout the eastern United States, but rarely in the South.

YELLOW HAWKWEED or KING DEVIL

Hieracium pratense—COMPOSITE FAMILY. A truly beautiful sight in the summer's bright sunshine are large stands of Hawkweed. However, they are a scourge to the farmer. It is a compact group of ½-inch flowers, several on each stem, growing from a bare main stem which rises from a basal rosette of leaves. The leaves are from 2 to 10 inches long and are covered with bristly hairs. Hawkweed grows from southern Ontario and Quebec through New England to Georgia, and west to Tennessee.

DEVIL'S PAINTBRUSH or ORANGE HAWKWEED

Hieracium aurantiacum—COMPOSITE FAMILY. Similar to the Yellow Hawkweed, the flowers are sometimes more red and orange, but are found in the same ecological and geographic locations. They bloom from early June through August. They also came from Europe.

ROUGH-FRUITED CINQUEFOIL
This plant was once considered an important source of medicine.

ROUGH-FRUITED CINQUEFOIL

Potentilla recta—ROSE FAMILY.   Unlike the Common Cinquefoil that blooms earlier and crawls over the ground, this is a tall plant, two feet or more in height, with hairy stems. The leaves are made up of 5 to 7 serrated leaflets. The yellow flowers have five petals and are up to 1 inch wide. It resembles the small wild rose to which it is related. A native of Europe, it is found growing from Quebec to North Carolina, and west to Missouri. It is found along roadsides as well as in fields.

BOUNCING BET

Saponaria officinalis—PINK FAMILY.   This is a tall plant reaching up to 2 feet. Its stem is coarse and smooth with elliptical leaves. The flowers are five-petaled, pink and white, and found on short stems near the top of the main stem. They are 1 inch wide and reflexed, sometimes double, and grow in thick clusters. They are found growing in waste places, even in town dumps. Its stems are jointed, which is a field mark of the pink family. This is an adventive. Its Latin name suggests soap because the juice in the stem foams up when mixed with water. It grows in most of temperate North America.

PASTURE ROSE

Rosa carolina—ROSE FAMILY. June is thought of as the month of roses (garden roses, that is) but fields, meadows, open spaces, and even roadsides have some lovely wild counterparts. This flower has the typical five petals of bright pink, 2 to 2½ inches across, multiple stamens, and is quite fragrant. It rarely grows more than 3 feet tall. The main branch has numerous smaller branches. The flowers are terminal on these branches, either singular or clustered. Its leaves are made up of five to seven leaflets. Like most roses it has sharp thorns. It is found from Maine across to Minnesota, and south to Florida and Texas.

RAGGED ROBIN

Lychnis flos-cuculi—PINK FAMILY. Again, a wanderer from Europe, but an attractive one to add to our collection of field plants. Its flowers are deep pink and tattered in appearance. It has five petals, and each petal appears to have been cut into a Y shape. Its stem is slender, up to 2 feet in height, with lance-shaped leaves growing out of the joints, indicating that it is a member of the pink family. It is found from Quebec through New England to New York and Pennsylvania.

Several members of the pink family are identified by notched petals jointed into a tube or a bladder. All start to bloom in June and continue into late summer.

BLADDER CAMPION

Silene cucubalus—PINK FAMILY. This plant will attract your attention with its inflated bladder below the calyx. The flower has five white petals, is about ¾ inch in diameter, and is found in loose clusters at the ends of small stems at the top of the main stem. The leaves are arranged opposite each other and are long and oval, up to 4 inches in length. This came from Europe, pos-

BLADDER CAMPION

The early basal leaves, when about 2 inches long, make a cooked green with a slightly bitter taste.

sibly as a garden flower, and escaped. It is found all across Canada to New Brunswick, and south to Virginia and Tennessee. It is found in fields and open places.

WHITE CAMPION

Lychnis alba—PINK FAMILY.   This flower has five petals, may be white or pink, and is about 1 inch wide. Its calyx is also inflated and veined. Its leaves and stem are covered with very fine hairs. It blooms at night, attracting night-flying moths. It starts to bloom late in the day, continuing through the night to the following day. Its leaves are lanceolate, up to 4 inches long. It grows in open, dry places ranging from Quebec to South Carolina, west to Alabama, and north to Missouri.

NIGHT-FLOWERING CATCHFLY

Silene noctiflora—PINK FAMILY.   It is very similar, except that the flowers are smaller, ¾ inch across, and its stems are covered with sticky hairs. It also has the same range.

WILD LUPINE

Lupinus perennis—PEA FAMILY.   Wild Lupine is a lover of sandy banks and open fields. The blue flowers are pealike, growing close together up the stem. It is about 14 inches tall. Its leaves are made up of oval or lanceolate leaflets radiating from the stem. It is found from Maine to Florida, west to Louisiana, and north to Minnesota. It should not be confused with the garden variety which often escapes.

EASTERN BLUE-EYED GRASS

Sisyrinchium atlanticum—IRIS FAMILY.   Various species of blue-eyed grass can be found blooming in June; this is the commonest. The flowers are about ½ inch across and have what appears to be six petals but actually are three blue petals and three blue sepals. The center of the flower is bright yellow. Each of the petals and sepals has a thornlike tip at the end. The flowers grow terminally on a grasslike stem. The leaves are also grasslike and are a soft green in color. They are often found in large masses in fields and on roadsides. They range throughout the whole area.

CHICKORY

Cichorium intybus—COMPOSITE FAMILY.   These lovely flowers brighten up the roadside, fields, and waste places with their sky-blue flowers. The stemless flowers grow directly from the sides of the stout, green main stem. The flowers are 1½ inches wide, with numerous long petals squared off at the top and toothed on the ends. Being a member of the composite family, they have two kinds of flowers, ray and disk, which are blue and fringed. The flowers bloom early in the morning and fade before the day is out, sometimes turning pink before they fold completely. The toothed leaves are found mostly at the base and are used for salads if picked before flowering. Its roots have been dried and ground and used as a coffee substitute. It is found all over the eastern United States. It is also an immigrant from Europe.

SELF-HEAL or HEAL-ALL

Prunella vulgaris—MINT FAMILY.   This, too, has blue flowers of an irregular shape. The individual flowers are irregular, and hooded, with the lower lip fringed and drooping. Many flowers are crowded on the end of the stem, which is from 6 to 12 inches long. The plant is often prostrate along the ground. Its name indicates that it was once used for medicine. It is found in open places, sterile ground, and along roadsides in all parts of the eastern United States. It was probably brought to the United States as one of the herbal medicines that the colonials used.

POKEWEED

Phytolacca americana—POKEWEED FAMILY.   It is a tall, coarse plant with red stems and can grow up to 10 feet. The flowers are actually white sepals, ¼ inch in diameter, growing in clusters from the junction of the leaf and stem. The leaves are elliptical, narrowing at both ends, and very large, from 4 to 20 inches long. They are found in clearings and roadsides. It ranges from Minnesota to Maine, and south. In the fall they produce quantities of dark-red berries which are poisonous, as is the rest of the plant. However, in the early spring, the early shoots, up to 6 inches tall, can be cooked and eaten like a vegetable. The red juice from the berries can also be used as a dye, and it was also used to color wine.

COW VETCH

Vicia cracca—PEA FAMILY.   Again an adventive from Europe. It is a vinelike plant about 2 to 3 feet long. The pealike flowers, ½ inch long, crowd together on one side of the stem. The flower stem grows out of the leaf junction on the main stem. The leaves

COW VETCH
This plant was introduced as a forage crop for cows.

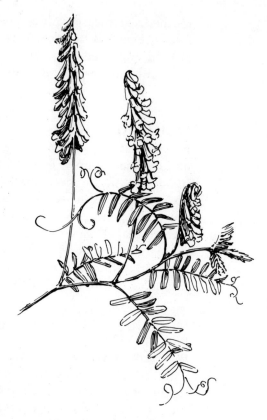

are compound, with eight to twelve pairs of leaflets, and end in a tendril. It is found in fields and roadsides from southern Canada to Virginia, and west to Illinois and Michigan.

BLACK-EYED SUSAN
Rudbeckia hirta—COMPOSITE FAMILY. Here is a flower to brighten up a summer's day, especially when seen en masse. Since it is a composite, it has two kinds of flowers. The outer or ray flowers are bright yellow, almost orange, and the disk flowers in the center are dark brown, about 3 inches in diameter. Its leaves and stem are quite hairy, and the leaves are oval, 2 to 7 inches in length. The plant itself is up to 3 feet tall. Native to the prairies, it moved eastward when the woodlands opened up. It is found all over the eastern United States.

16

FIELD FLOWERS

Midsummer—July

JULY BRINGS MANY INTERESTING WILDFLOWERS to the fields, roadsides, and sterile places, and along with them a host of insects that feed on them.

COMMON MILKWEED
Asclepias syriaca—MILKWEED FAMILY. There are a number of milkweeds, named so because of the milky sap which exudes when any part of the plant is broken. This is the one we are most apt to see. The flowers are small, ½ inch wide, with five turned-back petals in shades of pink, lavender, and brown. They are found in a terminal rounded cluster, or growing out of the junction of the leaf and stem. It is a tall, rugged plant, up to 6 feet or more, with large oval leaves, gray-green with hairy undersides. The seed pods are very interesting, 3 inches long and warty on the outside. When they open in the fall, each seed has a tiny parachute which carries it off into the wind. Although the mature plant is toxic, the early shoots are edible and can be used as a green vegetable. It is found growing from southern Canada to Georgia, and west to Iowa.

BUTTERFLY WEED
Asclepias tuberosa—MILKWEED FAMILY. A close relative, it has the same design, except it is more slender. Its flowers are brilliant orange. The leaves are narrow, as are the seed pods. It grows up to 2½ feet in height and is found in dry fields and roadsides. Because of its beauty, it has been introduced in the garden. It was once called Pleurisy Root because it was thought to cure lung ailments. It is found from southern Canada to Florida, west to Texas, and north to Minnesota. Unlike the milkweed plants, its fluid is clear and watery.

COMMON ST. JOHNSWORT
Hypericum perforatum—ST. JOHNSWORT FAMILY. There are many species of St. Johnswort but this is the one that you would be most apt to see. It was introduced from Europe. It is thought to

bloom on St. John's Day, hence the name. The flowers are up to 1 inch wide, bright yellow, with five petals in a perfect circle and numerous yellow stamens. The leaves are narrow or oblong, 1 to 2 inches long, and covered with translucent dots, a trademark of the St. Johnswort family. It grows up to 2½ feet tall and is found in fields and roadsides over most of the eastern United States.

Thistles are an obnoxious weed to the farmer, but their flowers are showy and large. There are about seventeen species in the area. They have a common characteristic: all are covered with spines.

COMMON THISTLE

Cirsium vulgare—COMPOSITE FAMILY.   It is found in fields, roadsides, and waste places. It is generally a tall plant, and can grow to 6 feet in height. The terminal flower heads are a large, compact group of purple-lavendar flowers, up to 3 inches in diameter. Its leaves are large, deeply serrated, and covered with spines. The main stem rises from a basal rosette of leaves. Like many of the field flowers it was probably brought over to this country because it was thought to have medicinal properties. Also the roots were once considered good eating.

COMMON THISTLE

This is the thorniest of thistles. Once it was used medicinally in treating varicose veins, earache, and toothache. The roots were also boiled and eaten.

COMMON MULLEIN

Verbascum thapsus—SNAPDRAGON FAMILY.   A group of these by the side of the road or in an open field is a spectacular sight. It has tall, woolly stems, over 6 feet, with bright-yellow, five-petaled, nearly regular flowers growing in tight clusters up the stem. The stem grows from a basal rosette of large gray-green oval leaves. It was probably brought from Europe because it was thought to have many medicinal qualities as well as other essential uses. The Quaker women used to rub their faces with the leaves to achieve a glow, since they were forbidden to use cosmetics. It is found from Maine to North Carolina, west to Iowa, and north to Minnesota.

SPREADING DOGBANE

Apocynum androsaemfolium—DOGBANE FAMILY.   This is another plant closely related to the milkweed. It is shrubby, with many branching stems, with numerous ⅓-inch-diameter, bell-shaped pink flowers at the ends. These flowers are quite fragrant. The stem, when broken, exudes a milky sap which was dried and chewed by the Indians. However, it is considered a poisonous plant. Indians also used the bark in the making of baskets and ropes. Its leaves are smooth, ovate, and blue-green, but the stems are reddish. It ranges throughout the eastern United States.

WHITE SWEET CLOVER

Melilotus alba—PEA FAMILY.   Standing up to 8 feet tall, it has small, white pealike flowers, ¼ inch long, growing in masses up a stem which comes from the junction of the leaf and the main stem. A bushy plant, its leaves are made up of three leaflets, lance-shaped and serrated. It was introduced from Europe where it was valued as a honey plant and for other properties. It is found throughout the eastern United States along roadsides, in fields, and in soil-poor areas.

The White Sweet Clover has a yellow counterpart—*Melilotus officinalis*, not quite as tall, but very similar in design and found in the same areas, often growing together. It is also a member of the pea family.

QUEEN ANNE'S LACE
Daucus carota—PARSLEY FAMILY.   This probably needs no introduction. A member of the parsley family, its flowers are creamy white, and sometimes there is a brownish flower in the center. It is rarely pink. It grows in a flat-topped cluster, from 3 to 5 inches in diameter, with very finely cut leaves, almost like ferns, growing alternately up the stem. It is considered a pest to the farmer but a delight to flower arrangers. It is named after Queen Anne, whose ladies wore the leaves in their hair. It is common all over the eastern United States, but not originally native.

ROUGH-FRUITED CINQUEFOIL
Potentilla recta—ROSE FAMILY.   This is often found in small patches along roadsides or in open fields. Its leaves are compound, five to seven leaflets growing radially from the stem. It is 1 to 2 feet tall and is found from Quebec to North Carolina, west to Missouri, and north to Minnesota. It, too, is not native.

PARTRIDGE PEA
Cassia fasciculata—PEA FAMILY.   It was named this because game birds feed on its seeds. Its flowers have five yellow petals, 1 to 1½ inches in diameter, and it grows up to 30 inches high. The flowers grow out of the main stem at the junction of the leaf and the stem. The leaves are compound, with ten to fifteen pairs of leaflets that close up at night. It ranges from New England to North Carolina, west to Tennessee, and north to Wisconsin.

WILD INDIGO
Baptisia tinctoria—PEA FAMILY.   A plant that is found in burned-over fields and dry sandy areas. Its flowers are small, pealike, and grow in terminal clusters. The leaves are palmate, compound with three leaflets, and bluish-green in color; as the summer wanes they turn black. It was once used as a dye. The leaves steeped in water were allowed to ferment to produce a blue dye. It ranges from southeastern Canada through New England to Florida, west to Louisiana, and north to Minnesota.

FIREWEED

Epilobium angustifolium—EVENING PRIMROSE FAMILY. Like the above, this has an affinity for burned-over areas and disturbed landscapes. The flowers grow in large groups and present a brilliant mass of bright lavender-red when in bloom. The flowers are four-petaled, growing toward the top of the main stem. The leaves are narrow, up to 8 inches long. It is said that the flowers covered large areas in England after the Second World War. It is found from Canada to the mountains of Maryland, North Carolina, and Tennessee, and west to South Dakota.

YARROW

Achillea millefolium—COMPOSITE FAMILY. This is a European flower that has found its way over here. Once used for medicines, it was imported and escaped as a field flower. It is a composite, but it does not resemble a daisy. Its flowers are tiny, ¼ inch in diameter, with four to six ray flowers that circle very tiny disk flowers. They grow in terminal flat clusters, and are a dirty-white shade, sometimes pink. Its leaves are up to 6 inches long, very finely serrated, and aromatic. It is found throughout the eastern half of the United States, and also on the western prairies.

BELLFLOWER or CREEPING BELLFLOWER

Campanula rapunculoides—BLUEBELL FAMILY. This is a tall plant often found growing by roadsides, waste places, and fields. Its beautiful blue, bell-shaped flowers are found growing up the main stem on one side, forming a flower head up to 3 inches tall. Leaves are elongated and heart-shaped. It was probably brought to this country as a garden flower but has escaped, and now ranges from Nova Scotia across to Minnesota, and south to Delaware and Ohio.

EVENING PRIMROSE

Oenothera biennis—EVENING PRIMROSE FAMILY. This is a plant of the fields, roadsides and waste places. It blooms from the end of

June well into fall. The interesting thing is that you might not see it in bloom. As the name suggests, it starts to bloom at twilight and closes as the day brightens, because its pollinators are night-flying moths. As the season progresses, however, it changes its blooming to daytime because when the blooms are open during the day, there is a yellow and pink night-flying moth that sleeps its day out in the blossom. The blooms are 1 to 2 inches across with four equal petals growing terminally in clusters at the end of the main stem. The plant is up to 5 feet tall. Its leaves are lanceolate, up to 8 inches long, and slightly serrated. It is found throughout the eastern half of the United States.

BIRDSFOOT TREFOIL
Lotus corniculatus—PEA FAMILY.   This is a plant that might catch your eye. It grows in masses along roadsides and in fields. Bright-yellow pealike flowers grow radially at the end of the stem and are ½ inch long. The compound leaves have five leaflets, three terminal and two at the base where the leaf joins the main stem. It is 6 to 25 inches tall. Its stems are weak, and often the plant is prostrate. Brought from Europe as a soil holder for roadside banks, it now ranges from Canada to North Carolina, and northwest to Ohio.

ELECAMPANE
Inula helenium—COMPOSITE FAMILY.   Like most members of the composite family, it has two kinds of flowers, ray and disk. Elecampane is very disorderly in appearance and has an unkempt look. Its yellow ray flowers are thin and stringy-looking and surround a darker disk. Its hairy stem is up to 6 feet tall, with large serrated leaves that may be up to 20 inches long clasping the stem. The undersides are fleecy. It was imported because it was thought to have medicinal properties. It ranges from southeastern Canada to North Carolina, west to Missouri, and north to Minnesota.

ASIATIC DAYFLOWER
Commelina communis—SPIDERWORT FAMILY.   It can be a pest in the garden because it grows in masses, and roots at leaf nodes. Its

flowers are small, ½ inch long, with two rounded blue petals and one white one. They are only open for one day. Its main stem is weak, more often than not trailing along the ground. Leaves are long and narrow, up to 5 inches in length, and clasp the stem. As the name suggests, the plant came from Asia. It ranges from Massachusetts to North Carolina and Alabama, to eastern Kansas, and north.

YELLOW GOATSBEARD

Tragopogon dubius—COMPOSITE FAMILY. Its yellow flower is similar to a dandelion but very flat, about 1 inch or more in diameter, and tall, with a smooth stem. The leaves are grasslike, broad at the base where they clasp the stem, but narrow as they lengthen, and can grow up to 1 foot in length. It is a fragile flower, which closes up before noon. It is said that the basal leaves can be eaten raw or cooked. It ranges from southern Maine to Virginia, west to Texas, and north to Illinois.

INDIAN TOBACCO

Lobelia inflata—BLUEBELL FAMILY. It is highly poisonous, even though the Indians used it for medicine and smoked it in their pipes. Its hairy stem is branched, with blue, irregular, ½-inch flowers growing out of a small leaf at the end of the branches, not closely spaced. The flowers have five petals, two growing upward and three growing downward. Under the flower is an inflated ovary. Its leaves are egg-shaped and toothed. It ranges from southern Ontario to Georgia, and west to eastern Kansas.

STEEPLEBUSH

Spiraea tomentosa—ROSE FAMILY. Looking at the plant, it does not look much like a rosebush. It is actually a shrub and perhaps should not be included here, but it is so often found in a field of wildflowers that it seems necessary to include it. It is an upright bush, 2 to 4 feet high, with tiny, pink, five-petaled roselike flowers, ¼ inch in diameter, growing in a compact spire up the stem. The stems are reddish-brown and wooly. Its leaves are 1 to 2 inches long, oblong, serrated, and have brownish hairs underneath. It ranges from southern Canada to Georgia, west to Arkansas, and northward.

MEADOWSWEET

Spiraea latifolia—Rose Family.   Like its cousin, the Steeplebush, it is a woody shrub. Its flowers are white or pinkish-white, ¼ inch in diameter, and have five petals. It grows in terminal compact clusters in a spirelike fashion. Its leaves can be up to 3 inches long, and are smooth and coarsely serrated. The undersides are pale green. It ranges from Newfoundland through New England to the mountains of North Carolina, and across to Michigan. It was once thought to have medicinal properties.

17

FIELD FLOWERS

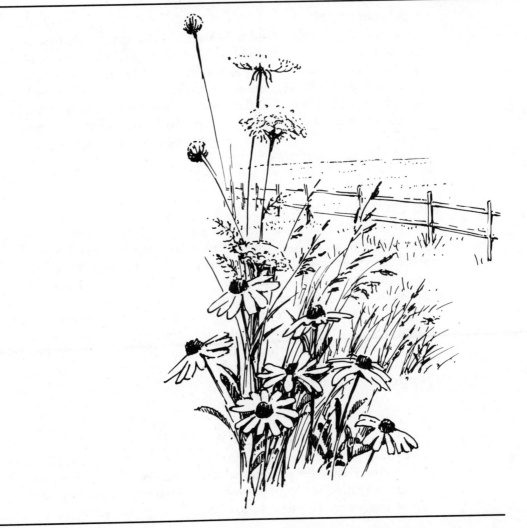

Late Summer

AUGUST HINTS THAT SUMMER MAY be coming to a close. The days are still hot, sometimes even the nights; yet the angle of the sun is lower, and the days are getting shorter. The parade of wildflowers moves across the fields and open places, and perhaps there will be more colors as the goldenrods and asters come into bloom, since they grow in masses.

COMMON TANSY

Tanacetum vulgare—COMPOSITE FAMILY. This was brought from Europe because it was thought to have many medicinal properties; however, it sometimes proved fatal. Unlike most members of the composite family, it has only disk flowers, about ½ inch wide, growing in a terminal flat-topped cluster on the main stem, which can reach 4 feet. Its leaves are 4 to 8 inches long and are deeply serrated. They have a very strong odor. It is well established all over the United States.

PEARLY EVERLASTING

Anaphalis margaritacea—COMPOSITE FAMILY. Its tiny white flowers are globular and look like a cluster of pearls at the end of the stem. The ¼-inch-wide disk flower has white bristles, or bracts, encircling the disk. It grows about 1 to 3 feet high, with leaves of greenish-white. Its leaves are long and narrow, up to 5 inches in length. Because they dry very nicely, they are often used in dried-flower arrangements. Male and female flowers are found on separate plants. It is found in open sandy places, fields, and roadsides. It ranges from Canada across the United States to North Carolina, and west to Kansas.

SWEET EVERLASTING or CUDWEED

Gnaphalium obtusifolium—COMPOSITE FAMILY. It is closely related to the Pearly Everlasting, which it somewhat resembles. Its flowers are found on small branches, in clusters growing near the top of the stem. The tiny yellow disk flowers are encircled by white or yellow bristles and bracts. It has a pleasant fragrance. Its leaves are narrow, pointed, and attached directly to the stem, which is greenish-white on top and woolly-white underneath. It is found throughout the eastern United States, and as far west as Texas.

JIMSONWEED
Datura stramonium—NIGHTSHADE FAMILY. This family includes tomatoes, but unlike tomatoes, Jimsonweed is highly poisonous. It is a tall, rugged plant, up to 5 feet, with a smooth stem. Its flowers are large white trumpets with five fused petals. The leaves are large, oval, and irregularly serrated. It was introduced from Central America and ranges throughout the whole area.

August is the time when goldenrod makes its appearance. There are about 100 species in the United States. This is strictly an American flower, although a few species have made their way into Europe. It is a much maligned plant because people associate it with hay fever, but goldenrod, unable to spread its pollen because it is sticky and cannot fly around, is not the culprit. It is the ragweed that blooms at the same time that is responsible.

EARLY GOLDENROD
Solidago juncea—COMPOSITE FAMILY. It is one of the first to bloom, sometimes as early as late July. Its flowers are tiny, with both yellow ray and disk flowers growing on branching stems near the top of the main stem. Its leaves are broadly lanced and sharply serrated. The stem is smooth and green. It grows 2 to 4 feet high, and is found from Nova Scotia to North Carolina, and west to Minnesota.

TALL GOLDENROD
Solidago altissima—COMPOSITE FAMILY. It is one of the most common goldenrods and also one of the tallest, sometimes reaching 7 feet. Its tiny yellow flowers are $\frac{1}{16}$ inch in diameter and are found on outward curving stems at the top of the main

stem. The slightly toothed leaves are long and narrow, rough on the upper side, but woolly underneath. Its range covers the eastern half of the United States as well as southern Canada.

SWEET GOLDENROD

Solidago odora—COMPOSITE FAMILY. As the name suggests, this goldenrod has anise-scented leaves which can be dried and used as a tea. It is a typical goldenrod. It is up to 3 feet tall. The leaves are long, narrow, and smooth, with tiny, transparent dots. The leaves are 4 inches long. The individual flower is very small and golden yellow. It ranges from New Hampshire southwest to Ohio, and south to Missouri.

SLENDER LADIES' TRESSES

Spiranthes gracilis—ORCHID FAMILY. You can find this growing in fields in August. The orchidlike flowers, white with a green throat, are very small—less than ½ inch long—and arranged spirally up a long, narrow stem, which rises from a basal rosette of oval or egg-shaped leaves. It ranges from Nova Scotia southwest to Texas, and north to Minnesota.

BLUE CURLS

Trichostema dichotomum—MINT FAMILY. This plant is very aptly named. Its blue flowers are almost circular in shape. Its four upper leaves are fused and curve downward, with blue stamens protruding from the upper petals in a perfect curve. Several flowers are found growing out of the end of the main stem. It grows from 4 to 14 inches tall and is found in open fields and along roadsides from southern Maine to Florida, west to Texas, and north to Minnesota.

POKE MILKWEED

Asclepias exaltata—MILKWEED FAMILY. You would hardly expect to find a milkweed growing in the woods or on the edge of the woods. Though it resembles the field variety, its clustered flowers droop from the junction of the leaf and the stem. The leaves are thin and pointed at both ends. It grows about 6 feet tall, with white, five-petaled flowers tinged with lavender or green. The petals are bent back and its stem is slender. It ranges from New Hampshire to North Carolina, west to Kentucky, and north to Michigan.

SMOOTH ASTER

Aster laevis,—COMPOSITE FAMILY.   This is an August-blooming aster found in the open fields and roadsides, growing up to 4 feet tall, with 1 inch flowers. The flowers have purple-blue ray flowers and yellow disk flowers. They are found terminally on short stems growing out from the end of the main stem, which is covered with a whitish bloom. The leaves are from 1 to 4 inches long, lance-shaped, and sometimes slightly rounded. The stems are smooth and thick. It is found from southern Canada to Georgia, west to Louisiana, and north to Kansas.

CALICO ASTER

Aster lateriflorus—COMPOSITE FAMILY.   This aster is attractive when growing en masse in a field. Its flowers are small, with white or lavender ray flowers and yellow and purple disk flowers. Numerous flowers grow on lateral branches that grow out near the top of the main stem. Its leaves are up to 6 inches long, lance-shaped, and coarsely serrated. It can grow up to 5 feet in height. It is common in fields and roadsides from Ontario to Georgia, west to Tennessee and Arkansas, and north to Minnesota.

18

FIELD FLOWERS

Autumn

SEPTEMBER SHOWS ALL THE SIGNS of things to come: leaves are starting to turn; many flowers have gone to seed; the days are cooler as well as shorter. But there are still flowers that are blooming in profusion.

FALL DANDELION

Leontodon autumnalis—COMPOSITE FAMILY.   This plant is apt to grow in large masses in mowed fields and roadsides. Its bright-yellow ray and disk flowers, 1 inch in diameter, are found terminally on a scaly stem that grows out of a basal rosette of leaves 5 or 6 inches long and deeply serrated. It ranges from southern Canada through New England to Pennsylvania. Unlike most of the later field flowers, it came from overseas.

SILVERROD

Solidago bicolor—COMPOSITE FAMILY.   Among the goldenrods there is a white one. Its tiny flowers are composed of white ray flowers and small, yellow disk flowers and are crowded on short stems growing out of a thin main stem. It has two leaf designs. The lower leaves are large, oval, and serrated, while the upper leaves are long, narrow, and smooth. It grows in open areas and along roadsides. It is found from southern Ontario to Georgia, west to Arkansas, and north to Wisconsin.

LANCE-LEAVED GOLDENROD

Solidago graminifolia—COMPOSITE FAMILY.   The Lance-leaved Goldenrod has tiny flowers arranged in flat-topped groups. The flowers are terminal on short branches growing out of the main stem. Its leaves are narrow and smooth, 3 to 5 inches long. It is common in fields and along roadsides from southern Canada to South Carolina, and west to South Dakota and Minnesota.

SHOWY GOLDENROD

Solidago speciosa—COMPOSITE FAMILY.   One of the most attractive of the goldenrods, it is a tall plant with a bright golden spire of flowers. The flowers themselves are small, ¼ inch wide, growing in tight masses at the end of a reddish stem. It grows about 6 feet tall. Its leaves are oval and serrated. It is found in open places, fields, and roadsides. It ranges from southern New Hampshire to North Carolina, west to Arkansas and Texas, and north to Minnesota.

There are many species of goldenrod and some crossbreed, making identification very difficult. Even the experts shy away from making positive identifications.

SICKLE-LEAFED ASTER

Chrysopsis falcata—COMPOSITE FAMILY.   One of several yellow asters, the flowers are asterlike except that both the ray and the disk flowers are yellow. Its leaves are narrow, curved, and stiff. It is found mostly in sandy open areas from Massachusetts to New Jersey.

RAGWEED

Ambrosia artemisiifolia—COMPOSITE FAMILY.   This is a plant with very few virtues. It is a primary cause of hay fever in the fall. Its flowers have no petals, only small drooping flower heads covered with pollen. The leaves are finely serrated. It grows in fields, roadsides, and waste places throughout the whole country.

Many of the field flowers extend their growing period into late fall and can be found blooming up to Thanksgiving if the season has been frost free. So take time through the seasons and watch the pageantry of the landscape as it evolves.

19

ROADSIDES

TAKE A SLOW RIDE ALONG back roads and byways, and you will be amazed by the number of wildflowers that can be seen from early spring to late fall and seem to be at home there. Actually, many roadsides are an extension of what is growing further in. Just about every kind of ecological situation can be found. However, many of the roadsides have been leveled or filled in and are often sandy. Since nature is quick to heal itself, if conditions are right, these sandy roadsides are soon covered with lichen and certain mosses, soon creating soil which will attract wildflowers that can subsist in this kind of environment.

Often roadsides have drainage ditches which attract aquatic plants that prefer to have their feet wet. Various forest trees are found at roadsides. Open fields often extend to the roadsides. River shores that the road may cross are cut through, leaving steep, sterile banks on either side.

Most of the plants that I will mention will have been described elsewhere in this book under each preferred ecological situation. Sandy roadsides probably are the first to bloom with small flowers, such as the Whitlow Grass.

WHITLOW GRASS
Draba verna—MUSTARD FAMILY.   It is barely 5 inches tall, with four white petals, ⅙ inch across. The petals are deeply notched, and it may look as if there are eight petals. You will have to stoop to see this one, but it is worth the effort. It blooms in March.

BLUETS
Houstonia caerulea—BEDSTRAW FAMILY.   These grow only up to 5 inches tall, with a delicate, blue-white, four-petaled flower ½ inch across, with a yellow center. Often it grows in drifts along the roadsides and even in lawns. This is enough to make you stop and take a look.

COMMON CINQUEFOIL
Potentilla simplex—ROSE FAMILY. This dainty flower indeed looks like a tiny rose. Its flowers have five petals and are bright

yellow, with five spreading leaflets. The plant is prostrate and creeps over the ground, ranging from Nova Scotia to Alabama and westward to Kansas and Minnesota.

BIRDFOOT VIOLET

Viola pedata—VIOLET FAMILY.   The flowers are in shades of lavender with an orange center. It has five petals, with two upward recurved petals and the other three pointed downward. The cinquefoil and the violet are often found growing together, making an interesting pattern on the roadside.

BIRDFOOT VIOLET

Its leaves are not the typical violet leaf but serrated and palmate and lacy in design. This is considered the most beautiful of the violets.

TRAILING ARBUTUS or MAYFLOWER

Epigaea repens—HEATH FAMILY.   On shady, sandy woodland banks, you may find this, the daintiest of all spring flowers. Its ½-inch, delicate, spicy-pink-white flowers are five-petaled, bell-shaped, and grow in clusters on trailing stems. The leaves are oval, up to 3 inches long, and hairy, a protection against the cool spring weather. These should never be picked or transplanted.

BLOODROOT
Sanguinaria canadensis—POPPY FAMILY. At the same time, along rich roadsides, we find the delicate bloodroot with its pure-white petals, 1½ inches across. There are eight to twelve petals on a bare stem with a deeply cleft leaf wrapped around the stem of the flower. Sometimes they grow in large masses of white, but should you break the stem or a leaf, a red sap will ooze out that will stain your hand and is very hard to rub off. You'll find them across Canada through New England and west to Texas.

CANADA MAYFLOWER
Maianthemum canadense—LILY FAMILY. This sometimes crawls out of the woods and carpets the roadsides. In case you don't remember, it is a small plant, 2 to 6 inches high, with a bare stem containing a cluster of tiny flowers which have four petals. Its range extends from Newfoundland south to the mountains of Georgia and westward to Iowa.

FRINGED POLYGALA
Polygala paucifolia—MILKWORT FAMILY. Inching out of a pine grove and down a sandy roadside, this odd-looking plant looks almost like an airplane. It has two lateral, purple-pink petals and a tube extending up from these petals with a fringe on the end. This plant is only 6 inches tall and has small egg-shaped green leaves. Its range extends across Canada south to Virginia and the mountains of Georgia, and west to Minnesota and Texas.

DANDELION
Taraxacum officinale—COMPOSITE FAMILY. Dandelions are an ubiquitous plant, growing almost everywhere, including roadsides, and are known to all by their bright-yellow compact flower heads. The deeply cleft leaves are found at the base of the flower stem in a basal rosette. They are edible.

BEARBERRY
Arctostaphylos uva-ursi—HEATH FAMILY. Another flower that has an affinity for sandy roadsides in May. It is an evergreen plant, trailing over the landscape with small leaves, ½ to 1 inch long.

The flowers are small, pinkish and bell-shaped, forming a tight cluster at the end of the stem. Bearberry was used in the making of tobacco. You'll find it in New England and south to Virginia and westward to Illinois.

As spring moves into summer, the roadsides really erupt. Most of the field flowers can be found along the roadsides. These flowers are taller in size. They dress the roadways from May to frost and beyond.

The clovers found along along the roads are the red, white, and rabbit's foot. Most clover blooms are constructed the same way. The individual flowers are small, compact, and somewhat rounded.

RED CLOVER

Trifolium pratense—Pea Family.   This one is about 6 inches to 2 feet tall. Its flower is a compact head of pinky-red about 1 inch long. It has three leaflets of two shades of green. It spreads over the ground by means of runners and is found throughout the United States.

RABBIT-FOOT CLOVER

Trifolium arvense—Pea Family.   Its flowers are about ¾ inch long. The individual flowers are grayish, pink, and furry. The leaves are slightly serrated at the tip. This plant has a special affinity for poor soil. It's found throughout the United States.

WILD LUPINE

Lupinus perennis—Pea Family.   This plant has beautiful flowers, pealike in design, growing up a tall, stout stem. Its leaves are compound, radiating from a central point. Lupines seem to have a preference for roadside banks and create a beautiful drift of blue from Maine to Florida and westward from Minnesota to Louisiana.

BLUE-EYED GRASS

Sisyrinchium montanum—Iris Family.   This plant is not as noticeable because the flowers are small, only ½ inch wide, blue, with three petals and three sepals which are also blue. Its leaves are grasslike. It can be found throughout the United States.

YELLOW HAWKWEED
Hieracium pratense—COMPOSITE FAMILY.   This is often found in large masses along superhighways as well as the back roads. Its flowers are much like dandelions, but smaller and flatter, and grow at the end of a long, thin stem. Its leaves are found around the base of the plant and are covered with hairs. There are several other closely related species, especially an orange-red one. You'll find it from southern Canada to Tennessee.

DAISY or OXEYE DAISY
Chrysanthemum leucanthemum—COMPOSITE FAMILY.   These grow along roadsides as well as in fields. Most people are acquainted with the stately, white circle of petals, ½ inch long, surrounding a tightly packed yellow disk. Its leaves are dark green and coarsely serrated. There is usually great temptation to pick a bouquet. This will do no harm because they are very common in the fields and along roadsides.

BLACK-EYED SUSAN
Rudbeckia hirta—COMPOSITE FAMILY.   Blooming a little later than the daisy, it originally lit up the open prairies and found its way to the East to grace our landscape. Like the daisy, it has a collar of bright yellow-orange petals around a dark-brown disk. It grows to a height of about 3 feet. Its leaves and stems are covered with stiff hairs.

More often than not, you will see an interesting combination growing together: mullein, chicory, and Queen Anne's lace.

COMMON MULLEIN
Verbascum thapsus—SNAPDRAGON FAMILY.   It is a tall, woolly plant, reaching up to 6 feet in height. Its flowers have five bright-

COMMON MULLEIN
A biennial whose woolly green leaves had many uses, including lamp wicks and insoles to keep feet warm.

yellow petals, 1 inch across, and run up a main stem which rises from a basal rosette of large gray-green, velvety leaves. Sometimes the mullein grows in masses by itself. It's found throughout the United States.

CHICORY
Cichorium intybus—COMPOSITE FAMILY.   It stands up to 4 feet tall with numerous square-tipped ray petals, 1½ inches wide. Its leaves are dandelionlike in design, only coarser.

QUEEN ANNE'S LACE

Daucus carota—PARSLEY FAMILY. It is a scourge to the farmer, but along the roadsides, its flat, white flowers only add beauty throughout the United States.

Two other plants that seem to favor roadsides came originally from Europe to be used medicinally and as garden plants and escaped: Yarrow and Tansy. However, neither are used very often for medicines today.

YARROW

Achillea millifolium—COMPOSITE FAMILY. The yarrow is a flat-topped gray-white plant, about 3 feet tall, made up of tiny flowerlets, ¼ inch across. The leaves are finely serrated and aromatic.

TANSY

Tanacetum vulgare—COMPOSITE FAMILY. Tansy is a bright-yellow, flat-topped flower made up of buttonlike flowerlets. It also has serrated, aromatic leaves.

Several members of the pink family brighten up our roadsides. Many of them came from Europe with the early settlers, escaped, and thrived.

BOUNCING BET

Saponaria officinalis—PINK FAMILY. The pink and white flowers, 1 inch across, are found in clusters at the end of the stem. They have five petals and are sweetly fragrant. The leaves are 2 to 3 inches long. The leaves, when crushed, release a fluid which will lather, hence the Latin name, meaning soap.

RAGGED ROBIN

Lychnis flos-cuculi—PINK FAMILY. These five-petaled flowers are deeply pink in color, deeply cut, and look as if they have been crushed before they bloomed. The flowers cluster at the end of the stem. The leaves are from 2 to 3 inches long, but get smaller as they approach the flower. It ranges from Quebec to Pennsylvania.

BLADDER CAMPION
Silene cucubalus—PINK FAMILY.   It has white flowers about 1 inch wide, with 5 petals, and looks as if it has a tiny balloon underneath the flower. The leaves are lanceolate and are wrapped around the flower. This plant grows up to 18 inches tall, from southern Canada to Tennessee and westward to Missouri.

Two plants of the pea family are utilized as soil holders along newly constructed roads.

BIRDSFOOT TREFOIL
Lotus corniculatus—PINK FAMILY.   This is a low-growing plant with bright-yellow flowers, pealike in design, growing around the top of the stem. The plant is 6 to 14 inches long but is found more often reclining on the ground. The oval leaves are about ½ inch long.

CROWN VETCH
Coronilla varia—PEA FAMILY.   The flowers are pink and white, again growing around the tip of the stem, which grows out of the junction of the leaf and the main stem. This plant also crawls over the ground. Both plants are found in large masses on roadsides from New England to Virginia and west to the Dakotas.

SPIDERWORT
Tradescantia virginiana—SPIDERWORT FAMILY.   Here and there on sandy banks, you might find this bright-blue flower with three petals, 1 inch across. The leaves are lanceolate and grasslike, growing out of a stem up to 4 feet tall. This plant is found from Rhode Island south.

BLUE CURLS

Trichostema dichotomum—Mint Family. Another blue flower found along sterile banks, its flowers are interesting. They are in two parts; the upper petal is divided into four, and the lower ones are recurved from the center of the flower. The four long stamens extend to form a circle. The leaves are narrow, oblong to lanceolate, ¾ to 2½ inches long. Although most plants are small, about 6 inches tall, they can range up to 24 inches. They are found from Maine to Florida.

BUTTERFLY WEED

Asclepias tuberosa—Milkweed Family. A really bright plant that will attract your eye along about the middle of summer and also grows along grassy roadsides is this orange flower. Butterfly Weed is about 1 to 2½ feet tall, with a cluster of flowers 2 inches across, made up of individual flowerlets about ⅜ inch across with five recurved petals. The leaves are oblong and narrow, up to 5 inches long. Its fruit is a typical milkweed pod. It was once thought to be a cure for lung diseases. You'll find it from southern Canada to Florida and westward to Texas and Minnesota.

The roadsides from July until the frost and even later are a colorful array of two genera of plants, the asters and the goldenrods. The individual aster flowers are small daisylike flowers coming in many colors, from white to pink and purple. There is even a yellow one. They, like the goldenrods, have their seasons, one following the other. In all there are about 250 species of asters in North America. Some of the flowers are only ¼ inch in diameter. Some grow in clusters on the main stem, while others grow singularly on the stem. They range in height from 1 to more than 4 feet.

Along with the asters in the same growing season are the many species of goldenrods whose trademarks are wandlike flowerheads scattered up the stem. Like the aster, it is a composite. The individual flowers are small, some only ⅙ inch in diameter. The plant, however, is a tall one, with some growing over 6 feet. Its leaves are often lanceolate; some are even broader-leafed. There are up to 100 species in North America. However, many hybridize, so that they are hard to identify.

In wet ditches are a number flowers mentioned previously. In June the irislike Blue Flag appears. It is a large flower, about 4 inches long, with three upright petals and three blue sepals which recurve downward. Sometimes it grows in large masses but often it is found in artistic clumps. Its leaves are long and straplike. It can be found from Nova Scotia to Virginia and westward to Ohio.

JEWELWEED

Impatiens capensis—TOUCH-ME-NOT FAMILY.   Another lover of damp and wet places is this dainty plant. It is a tall, fleshy plant with semitransparent leaves. The flowers are downward-hanging and bell-shaped, with a long spur at the bottom of the flowers. The fascinating thing about this plant is its long, green seed capsule which explodes when ripe, scattering its seed all around. It's found from Canada to Georgia and westward to Oklahoma.

BONESET

Eupatorium perfoliatum—COMPOSITE FAMILY.   Later on in August there are a number of wildflowers that like the wet places along the roadsides. Most are tall, for they have had the summer in which to grow. This one is a flat-topped plant of grayish-white, made up of a cluster of ¼-inch flowers. The leaves are from 4 to 8 inches long, jointed together with the main stem growing through them. This was once thought useful in setting broken bones, hence the name.

JOE-PYE WEED

Eupatorium maculatum—COMPOSITE FAMILY.   This often grows along with Boneset and in masses. It grows up to 6 feet tall, or more, with a cluster of tiny purple flowers at the end of the main stem. The leaves are 4 to 8 inches long and grow in whorls around the stem. Again, it was thought to have wonderful healing powers. It ranges from Canada to Florida and west to Texas.

CARDINAL FLOWER

Lobelia cardinalis—BLUEBELL FAMILY. This sometimes grows among the Boneset and Joe-Pye-Weed. Its tall, red spikes will surely make you stop and investigate. The flowers are tubular, 1½ inches long, with the tube cut into lobes: two on the upper side of the flower, and three on the lower. Its leaves are 6 inches long and lanceolate. Like the others, it is a tall plant, up to 4 feet and over.

TURTLEHEAD

Chelone glabra—SNAPDRAGON FAMILY. This also might be found in company of the above, making a fascinating composition in color and design. I once found it beside a much-traveled super-highway. The plant is about 3 feet tall with rather interesting flowers resembling a turtle, as the name implies. The white flowers are found terminally on the main stem in clusters which are about 1 to 1½ inches long. The leaves are 3 to 6 inches long, lanceolate and sharply serrated. It ranges from southern Canada to Georgia and west to Missouri.

ARROWHEAD

Sagittaria latifolia—WATER PLANTAIN FAMILY. Often in a drainage ditch where there is a little standing water, you will find the Arrowhead, so named for its leaves. It has three-petaled white flowers growing around the stem, which rises from a basal rosette of large arrow-shaped leaves up to 16 inches in length. It is a tall plant, up to 4 feet tall. Its starchy tubers were once eaten by the Indians.

As you ride along you may find others that you may have seen in the woods, fields, or wet places. Once I found a Lady's Slipper growing right by the roadside flush to the pavement. You may discover similar jewels of delight on your own wildflower journeys.

BIBLIOGRAPHY

Blachan, Neltje. *Nature's Garden*. New York: Doubleday, Page and Co., 1900.

Britton, Nathaniel Lord, and Hon. Addison Brown. *An Illustrated Flora of the Northern United States and Canada*. New York and London: Hafner Publishing Co., 1963.

Coon, Nelson. *Using Plants for Healing*. Hearthside Press, 1963.

Dana, Mrs. William Starr. *How to Know the Wildflowers*. New York: Scribner's, 1895; Dover, 1963.

Dwelly, Marilyn J. *Wildflowers of New England, Spring Edition*. Camden, Maine: Down East Enterprises, 1973.

Godfrey, Michael. *Sierra Club Illustrated Guide: The Piedmont Region*. San Francisco: Sierra Club Books, 1980.

Headstrom, Richard. *Suburban Wildflowers*. New York: Prentice-Hall, 1984.

Hotchkiss, Neil. *Common Marsh, Underwater, and Floating Leaved Plants of United States and Canada*. New York: Dover, 1972.

House, Homer. *Wildflowers*. New York: Macmillan, 1967.

Jorgensen, Neil. *Sierra Club Naturalist's Guide: Southern New England*. San Francisco: Sierra Club Books, 1980.

BIBLIOGRAPHY

Kingsbury, John M. *Deadly Harvest.* New York: Holt, Rinehart & Winston, 1965.

Klimas, John E., and James A. Cunningham. *Wildflowers of Eastern America.* New York: Knopf, 1974.

Magrue, Dennis W. *Freshwater Wetlands: Guide to Common Indication Plants of the Northeast.* Amherst, Mass.: University of Massachusetts Press, 1981.

Newcomb, Lawrence. *Newcomb's Wildflower Guide.* Boston: Little, Brown, 1977.

Niering, William A., and Nancy C. Olmstead. *The Audubon Society Field Guide to North American Wildflowers (Eastern Region).* New York: Knopf, 1979.

Norman, Marcia Gaylord, and Harriet Weil Hubbell. *Treasures of the Shore, a Beachcomber's Botany.* Chatham Conservation Foundation, 1963.

Peterson, Roger Tory, and Margaret McKenny. *Field Guide to Wildflowers.* Boston: Houghton Mifflin, 1968.

Petrie, Loren C., and Marcia G. Norman. *A Beachcomber's Botany.* Chatham, Mass.: Chatham Conservation Foundation, 1968.

Scott, Jane. *Botany in the Field.* New York: Prentice-Hall, 1984.

Woodworth, Carol, and Harold Rickets. *Common Wildflowers of Northeastern United States.* Woodbury, N.Y.: Barron's, 1979.

INDEX

Alsike Clover, 109–110
Altitude, effect on flower growth, 2
Anemone, Wood, 43–44
Annual Saltmarsh Aster, 36
Aquatic plants, 96–101, 144
Arbutus, 42, 143
Arrowhead, 97–99, 152
Asiatic Dayflower, 127–128
Asters, 13, 29–30, 35–36, 64–65, 91–92,
    135, 139
Autumn flowers, 138–139

Baneberry, 46
Beach Heather, 24
Beach Pea, 18
Beach Plum, 19
Beaches: 16–22; bogs, 24–31; dunes, 24;
    salt marshes, 34–39; sea beach flow-
    ers, 16–22
Bearberry, 144–145
Beechdrops, 69
Bellflower, 126
Bellwort, 45
Benzoin, 74–75
Birthwort, 39
Black Mustard, 6
Bladder Campion, 116
Bloodroot, 143, 144
Blooming time: factors affecting, 2–3;
    water plants and land plants, 96; See
    also specific subject headings
Blue Curls, 134, 150
Blue-Eyed Grass, 145–146
Blue Flag, 78
Bluets, 105, 142
Bogbean, 96
Bogs, 24–31
    wet acid soil, effect, 24
Boneset, 90, 151
Bottle Gentian, 93
Bouncing Bet, 115–116, 148
Brooks, flowers growing in, 96–101
Buckbean, 96
Bunchberry, 58–59
Bur Reed, 81–82

Butter-and-Eggs, 12, 110
Buttercup, 109
Butterfly Weed, 122, 150–151

Calico Aster, 135
Campion, 117, 149
Canada Lily, 85
Canada Mayflower, 50, 139, 143
Cardinal Flower, 88, 152
Celandine, 13, 74
Chickweed, 111
Chicory, 8, 118, 147
Cinquefoil, 108, 115, 125, 142–143
Cities: wildflowers found growing in,
    6–14; soil conditions, 6
Climbing Boneset, 90–91
Clintonia, 46
Closed Gentian, 93
Clover, 11, 105, 109–110, 124, 125
Cold, effect on flower growth, 2
Colicroot, 81
Coltsfoot, 74
Common Bladderwort, 101
Common Blue Violet, 44–45, 106
Common Burdock, 9
Common Chickweed, 111
Common Cinquefoil, 108, 142–143
Common Mullein, 7, 124, 146–147
Common Saltwort, 17
Common Tansy, 7–8, 132
Common Thistle, 123
Compound leaves, 4
Cow Parsnip, 79
Cow Vetch, 119–120
Cow Wheat, 59
Cranberry, 25
Creeping Bellflower, 126
Crown Vetch, 149
Cudweed, 132–133
Curly Dock, 12
Cypress Spurge, 105

Daisy, 111, 144, 146
Dandelion, 6, 104–105, 139, 144
Deer Grass, 81

Dryness: effect on growth, 2; mid-summer, 78–85
Dusty Miller, 19–20

Early Field Goldenrod, 133
Early Meadow Rue, 73
Early Saxifrage, 52
Early spring flowers, 42–53
Early summer field flowers, 107–111
Eastern Blue-Eyed Grass, 119
Ecological areas or habitats, emphasis on, 2
Elecampane, 127
Equipment needed for wildflower identification, 3–4
Evening Lychnis, 9
Evening Primrose, 13, 126–127
Everlasting Pearly, 132

False Heather, 24
False Hellebore, 73
False Solomon's Seal, 46
Featherfoil, 100
Fern-Leaved Foxglove, 61
Field flowers: adaptability, 104; autumn, 138–139; early summer, 107–111; farming, effect, 104; grasses, 104; late summer, 131–135; midsummer, 114–129; soil in fields, effect, 104; spring flowers, 104
Fireweed, 126
Fleabane, 37, 111
Floating Heart, 99
Foxglove, 60–61
Fresh water: flowers growing in, 96–101; blooming time of land plants compared, 96
Fringed Gentian, 93
Fringed Polygala, 52, 144

Gaywings, 52
Gentian, 93
Geranium, 51
Glasswort, 36–37
Golden Alexanders, 75
Golden Club, 97
Golden Ragwort, 73–74
Goldenrod, 21, 30, 65, 91, 139; early, 133; sweet, 134; tall, 134
Grass Pink, 27
Grasses: fields, in, 104; *See also* specific names
Great Lobelia, 88
Groundnut, 93

Harebell, 85
Hawkweed, 114, 146

Heal-All, 119
Heat: effect on growth, 2; effect on woodland-growing flowers, 56, 64
Hepatica, 43
Horned Poppy, 39
Horseweed, 13

Identification of wildflowers, equipment needed, 3–4
Indian Cucumber Root, 51
Indian Pipes, 65–66
Indian Tobacco, 129

Jack-in-the-Pulpit, 47–48
Jerusalem Artichoke, 94
Jewelweed, 80, 151
Jimsonweed, 133
Joe-Pye-Weed, 89, 151
Jointweed, 22

King Devil, 114

Lady's Slipper, 56–57
Ladies' Tresses, 27, 92–93, 134
Lambkill, 83–84
Lance-Leaved Goldenrod, 91, 138
Lance-Leaved Violet, 24
Land plants: blooming time compared with plants growing in fresh water, 96
Large Flowered Trillium, 48
Late summer flowers: field, 131–135; wetlands, 88–94; woodlands, 64–69
Latitude, effect, 2
Leaves described, 4
Lilies, 44, 60, 84–85, 96–97, 98–100
Liverleaf, 43
Lobelia, 88, 101
Lupine, 145

Marsh Elder, 34
Marsh Marigold, 72
Marsh Rosemary, 34
Marsh St. Johnswort, 83
Marshes, generally: midsummer flowers, 78–85; salt marsh flowers, 34–39
Mayflower, 42, 50, 139
Meadow Beauty, 81
Meadows, spring flowers in, 78–85
Meadowsweet, 129
Midsummer flowers: field: July, 122–129; June, 114–120; wetlands, 78–85; woodlands, 56–61
Milkweed, 9, 122, 134
Milkwort: Cross-Leaved, 30
Monkey Flower, 80–81
Mullein, 7, 124, 146–147

Narrow Leaved Cattail, 37
New England Aster, 91
New York Aster, 92
New York Ironweed, 89
Night Flowering Catchfly, 118
Nodding Ladies' Tresses, 92–93
Northern False Foxglove, 60
Nodding Trillium, 48

Open fields, flowers growing in, 104–139;
    See also Field flowers; specific subject
    headings
Orach, 17
Orange Hawkweed, 114
Oxeye Daisy, 114

Palmate leaves, 4
Partridge Pea, 125
Parts of flowers, 3
Pasture Rose, 116
Pepper Grass, 10
Petals described, 3
Pickerelweed, 98
Pinewood, 31
Pink Knotwood, 13
Pink Ladies' Slipper, 56
Pipewort, 100–101
Pipsissewa, 59–60
Pitcher Plant, 27–28
Plant families, 3; described, 3–4
Plant press, use of, 3
Plantains, 37–38, 66–67, 98, 111
Pogonia, 26–27, 57
Poke Milkweed, 134
Pokeweed, 119
Ponds, flowers growing in, 96–101
Prickly Lettuce, 11
Prickly Pear, 21–22
Prince's Pine, 59–60
Purple Aster, 65
Purple Bladderwort, 101
Purple Gerardia, 28–29
Pussy Toes, 106

Queen Anne's Lace, 12, 125, 128

Rabbit-Foot Clover, 145
Ragged Robin, 116, 149
Rainfall, effect on growth, 2
Rattlesnake Plantain, 66–67
Red Baneberry, 46
Red Clover, 105, 145
Roadside: flowers growing at, 142–143;
    aquatic plants, 142
Robin's Plantain, 111
Rose Pogonia, 26–27

Roseroot, 39
Roses, 20, 116
Rough-Fruited Cinquefoil, 115, 125

St. Johnswort, 122–123
Salt marshes: Asters, 36; flowers, 34–39;
    grasses found in, 34; tides, effect,
    34–39
Samphire, 36–37
Sarsaparilla, 50
Saxifrage, 52
Scarlet Pimpernel, 39
Sea beach flowers, 16–22; soil makeup,
    effect, 16; water needs, 16
Sea Blite, 18
Sea Lavender, 34
Sea Pink, 36
Sea Rocket, 16
Seabeach Orach, 17
Seaside Goldenrod, 20
Seaside Plantain, 37–38
Seaside Spurge, 17
Self-Heal, 119
Sepals described, 3
Sessile leaves, 4
Sheep Laurel, 83–84
Shinleaf, 59
Showy Goldenrod, 138
Sickle-Leafed Aster, 139
Silverrod, 65, 138
Silverweed, 36
Skunk Cabbage, 72
Slender Blue Flag, 79
Slender Ladies' Tresses, 134
Smartweed, 13
Smooth Asters, 64, 135
Smooth Sumac, 12
Soil, effect, 2; acidity, 42; alkalinity, 42
Solomon's Seal, 45–46
Spatterdock, 100
Spearscale, 17
Spicebush, 74–75
Spotted Cowbane, 79
Spotted Wintergreen, 60
Spreading Dogbane, 124
Spring Beauty, 52
Spring flowers: field, 104–106; wetlands,
    72–75; woodlands, 42–53
Star-Flowered False Solomon's Seal, 30
Steeplebush, 128–129
Strawberry, 108
Structure of flowers, 3
Sundew, 28
Swamp Rose Mallow, 34–35, 89
Swamp Saxifrage, 75
Sweet Everlasting, 132–133
Sweet White Violets, 47, 75

Tall Buttercup, 109
Tall Goldenrod, 133–134
Tall Meadow Rue, 79
Tansy, 108, 132, 148–149
Thistle, 7–8, 10, 39, 123
Thread-Leaved Goldenrod, 30
Trailing Arbutus, 42, 143
Trillium, 48–49
Trout Lily, 44
Turk's Cap Lily, 84
Turtlehead, 88–89, 152

Urban wildflowers, 6–14
  soil, effect, 6

Vetch, 119–120, 149
Violets, 44–45, 47, 106, 109, 143
Virgin's Bower, 91

Wake Robin, 49
Water Hemlock, 79
Water Lily, 98–99
Water Lobelia, 101
Water Plantain, 98
Wetlands: flowers found in late summer,
  88–94; mid-summer, 78–85; spring,
  72–75
White Baneberry, 46
White Campion, 9, 117
White Clover, 9
White Fringed Orchid, 82–83

White Lettuce, 69
White Swamp Azalea, 83
White Sweet Clover, 11, 124
White Wood Aster, 64
Whitlow Grass, 104, 142
Whorled Loosestrife, 58
Whorled Pogonia, 57
Wild Calla Lily, 96–97
Wild Columbine, 48
Wild Geranium, 50
Wild Indigo, 125
Wild Lupine, 118
Wild Sarsaparilla, 50
Windflower, 43–44
Wintergreen, 67–68
Wood Anemone, 43–44
Wood Lily, 60
Woodland Sunflower, 68
Woodland flowers: early spring, 42–43;
  late summer, 64–69; mid-summer,
  56–61
Wrinkled Rose, 20

Yarrow, 7, 126, 148
Yellow-Eyed Grass, 26
Yellow Goatsbeard, 128
Yellow Hawkweed, 11
Yellow Pond Lily, 100
Yellow Lady's Slipper, 56–57
Yellow Sweet Clover, 11
Yellow Thistle, 39